Kids Can Dig It

Session	Theme	Kids Dig the Bible	Kids...	
Kickoff	Full of treasures	Matthew 6:21 We treasure the Bible.	Treasure Chest; Treasure Picture Frames; Trash to Treasure; Bible Acrostic	Treasure Hunt; Treasure, Treasure So High; Prui
1	Rolls of scrolls	2 Kings 22:1-13; 23:1-3 We discover the Old Testament.	Biscuit Bible Scrolls; Make a Scroll; Phylacteries; Copycat Scribes	Hide and Seek; Carry God's Message; Josiah Says; Mirror Game
2	Walking with Jesus	Luke 4:16-21 We discover the New Testament.	Bible Books Poster; Letter Pouch; Good Newspaper; Codex	Keep It Up; Dropped a Letter; Reorder the Books; Good News Tag
3	Messages in the Bible	Genesis, Judges, Matthew, Acts We explore the story of God's people in the Bible.	Printing Blocks; God's Word is Like; Bible Messages; Decode the Messages	God's Word Spreads; Secret Church Sardines; Old or New?; Prisoner's Base
4	A library in one book	Psalm 119:9 We discover different types of writing in the Bible.	Bible Brownies; Fill in the Books; Books of the Bible Bookmark; Making Papyrus	Books of the Bible Memory Game; Bible Books Upset; What Category; Story Blanket
5	God's promises	Genesis 6:18; 9:11; 12:2-7; Jeremiah 29:11; 31:31-34 We discover God's promises to us in the Bible.	Promise Cans; Rainbow Mobile; Illuminate Psalm 23; Star Promise Bracelet	Pass the Bible; Lighthouse; Promiseball; God Loves
6	Life in Bible times	Luke 10:30-35 We imagine life in Bible times.	Bible Character Sculpture; Egg Carton Scavenger Hunt; Make a Map; Friendship Bracelets	Nomads and Settlers; Shepherd Relay; Boat Tag
7	Words in our hearts	Matthew 7:24-27 We listen to God's word and keep it in our hearts.	Mezuzahs; Plant Seeds; Words in My Heart; Shema Door Hanger	Talent Charades; Rock, Sand, Rain; Listen Closely!; Stick to the Heart Tag
8	Guiding light	Matthew 5:14-16 The Bible lights our way.	Candle Holders; Stained-Glass Artwork; Simple Beeswax Candles; Clay Lamps	Light Labyrinth; Dark Draw; Flashlight Tag; Spooky Scavenger Hunt
Closing Celebration	Celebrating the Bible (Simchat Torah)	Nehemiah 8:1-18 We celebrate the gift of God's word.		

KIDS CAN DIG THE BIBLE

Copyright © 2010 by Faith & Life Resources, a division of Mennonite Publishing
Network, Scottdale, PA 15683 and Waterloo, ON N2L 6H7.

The following titles were used in the writing of *Kids Can Dig the Bible*:
- Stutzman, Rose Mary, editor. *The Bible: Digging for Treasure*. Vacation Bible
  School. Scottdale, PA: Herald Press, 2000.
- *Venture Clubs: Exploring God's Way*. Newton, KS: Faith & Life Press,
  1999—2005.

Unless otherwise noted, Scripture text is quoted, with permission, from the *New Re-
vised Standard Version Bible*, copyright 1989, by the Division of Christian Education
of the National Council of the Church of Christ in the United States of America.

International Standard Book Number: 978-0-8361-9529-3
Edited by Rebecca Seiling, Eleanor Snyder, Mary Ann Weber;
design by Reuben Graham
Printed in the USA

To order or request information, please call 1-800-245-7894 in the U.S. or 1-800-
631-6353 in Canada.

www.mennomedia.org

Kids Can Dig the Bible
Table of Contents

Getting Started
About the Theme

Kids Can Dig the Bible invites children to dig into and discover the rich treasures in the Bible. Although the Bible was written thousands of years ago, it continues to speak today. It guides us and teaches us how to live in God's way. The Bible stories show how we can have a relationship with God and each other. Through the stories of God's people, we discover how their story is our story too.

We come to the Bible with many experiences. Some of us are familiar with the stories and teachings; others are just beginning to learn. The deeper we dig into the Bible, the more treasures we can find.

In these sessions, you and the children will learn more about the biblical story. As you tell the Bible stories included in this series, have your own Bible open and accessible. Whenever you can, show the children how to find the stories and memory verses. Share your interest in the Bible, and the children will catch it.

About the children

This curriculum is for six- to ten-year-old children, but can be adapted for other ages. What are these children like? If you are a parent or teacher, you know that children come in all shapes and sizes. Each one is unique. God's creativity is imprinted on each child. **As you get to know the children as individuals, remember that children**
- learn in different ways
- learn best by experiencing, seeing, discovering, and doing
- have different reading abilities
- are beginning to develop abstract thinking skills
- like to move around and be active
- respond well to loving and caring adult models they can trust and follow
- like to have friends and be friends
- can be exclusive in their friendships and often have a best friend
- have a strong sense of fairness, of right and wrong
- are already in relationship with God, even though they may not have language for their relationship
- are beginning to ask questions and need a safe environment to do so
- thrive when treated with love, respect, and compassion

About the leaders

Children's experiences of faith are memorable due in part to the leaders who guide them. **Leaders who work with children**
- model God's love, forgiveness, and care for everyone
- are mature youth or adults who always act as adults
- do not see themselves as buddies to the children, but guides
- love children
- are energetic and enthusiastic
- have a passion for peacemaking
- have good conflict resolution skills
- see that children are safe at all times

Gifts of leadership needed

- **Music:** Choose songs and lead the singing.
- **Kids Talk Peace:** Tell Bible stories and/or work with children to present the readers theaters or Bible skits, and lead in faith conversations.
- **Kids Create:** Decide on the craft activities that will be offered; gather materials, and work with the children on a handcraft that they will take home with them. Find helpers to work with children or lead a group if you plan more than one activity.
- **Kids Move:** Lead the games and talk about how they fit in with the theme.
- **Group leaders:** Adults or mature youth whose main role is to build relationships with a small group of children (up to ten children per group).
- **Memory tutors (optional):** an adult who is willing to work one-on-one with children to learn memory verses.
- **Prayer pals (optional):** an adult matched with a child so that they can pray for each other. Invite the pals to join you for the closing celebration.

About the session format

The curriculum

- is geared to children in grades one through five
- can be used with multi-age groups or separate younger and older groups
- can be adapted for kindergarten children or junior youth
- includes plans for sessions that last forty-five minutes to an hour
- includes time for gathering, singing, Bible story and discussion, crafts, and games
- includes ten complete sessions: kickoff session to introduce theme, eight peace-related topics, and a final celebration event
- includes resource/reference pages with ideas for opening and closing activities, memory verses and tips for memorizing, snacks, book list, additional craft ideas, service projects, and how to manage unwanted behavior
- includes lots of suggestions for crafts and games for each session.

Suggested times during each session

Kids Cluster (5 minutes)

- suggestions for early arrivals, singing, memory review

Kids Talk Peace (10 minutes)

- introduction to theme, Bible story, reflection, and conversation starters

Kids Create and Kids Move (20 to 35 minutes)

- suggestions for activities, crafts, and/or games

Closing (5 minutes), optional

- gathering time ideas for closing blessing and ending rituals

Resources
Kids Cluster

Depending on the setup, children may come to club at different times. Be ready by having a variety of activities in which to engage children as they arrive, helping to prevent unwanted behavior. When most of the children have arrived, or at the starting time, begin the session.

SUGGESTIONS FOR EARLY ARRIVALS
1. **First session:** Make personal name tags.
2. **Bible mural:** Create a mural where children can draw or glue pictures of Bible stories.
3. **Question box:** Make a box with an opening on top. Children may have questions about the Bible and can write them on paper and put the paper in the box.
4. **Puzzles:** Younger children may enjoy putting together a puzzle. Find one that has a scene from the Bible.
5. **Bible books:** Set up a Bible book corner with children's story Bibles or children's books about the Bible. See page 13 for a book list. Read and talk together about the stories.
6. **Play dough or building blocks:** Build or create objects or characters from favorite Bible stories.
7. **Practice memory verses** with a memory ball or by using the creative ideas found on page 12.

GROUP-BUILDING IDEAS
Children may not know each other, even if they go to the same school or church, so plan get-acquainted games.
1. **Find a partner.** Give the pairs one minute to talk to each other. The children will introduce their partner to the larger group and share one thing learned about him or her.
2. **Each child will tell her or his name** and a favorite food that begins with the same letter as their name. For example, "I'm Sandi and I like spaghetti."
3. **Play a "line-up" game.** Children line up according to their age, month of birthday, or size (smallest to tallest).
4. **Celebrate how God created us each differently.** Give the children two characteristics, and ask them to arrange themselves depending on which of the characteristics they are most like. Say, "If you are most like the first word, move to my right. If you are most like the second word, move to my left." For each characteristic, use the lead-in "I am . . . " Here are some possible pairs: quiet/noisy, leader/follower, messy/neat, cat/dog, and rabbit/turtle.
5. **Distribute about five colored stickers** or color-coated chocolate candies randomly to each child. For each different color, assign a topic about which the children will share. For example, a yellow candy topic might be a favorite school subject or game, and a red candy topic might be a favorite hobby.

6. **"Finish this sentence" cards.** Create cards with sentence starters. Children choose a card and must finish the sentence: My favorite color is . . . A quality of a best friend is . . .

7. **Play a category game.** Place topic names on slips of paper that represent categories such as plants, animals, countries, and colors. Children take turns pulling a slip out of a basket and see how many items they can name that fit into the category.

CLOSING

This is a time to send the children out into their daily lives with a word or sentence encouraging them to remember the Bible stories at home, school, and wherever they go. Be sure you send any announcements, crafts, and other items home with the children.

The following are closing-time suggestions:
1. **Gather in the large group,** or plan for a simple closing at the end of the last activity.
2. **Use a spoken blessing** (see numbers 1 and 2 below), along with the motions.
3. **Offer a short, closing prayer.**
4. **Give a short blessing for each session** (see number 3 below).

1. Go in God's Word
(Stand together in a circle facing each other.)
Go in the light of God's word. *(open palms in front as if you are holding a book)*
The word of love, *(cross arms over chest)*
The word of peace, *(join hands with each other)*
The word of truth. *(look up, raise joined hands overhead)*

2. Corinthians 13:13
(Stand together in a circle facing each other.)
The grace of the Lord Jesus Christ, *(fold hands together in prayer gesture)*
the love of God, *(cross arms in front of body)*
and the communion of the Holy Spirit *(raise open hands to the side)*
be with all of you. *(join hands together)*

3. Sending Blessings
Kick off session: "Go in God's love, ready to discover the treasures in the Bible."
Session 1: "You are part of God's good creation. Go in God's peace and love."
Session 2: "May God's good news inspire you to make good choices."
Session 3: "God's message is for you! Go in God's love."
Session 4: "May God write a letter of love on your heart."
Session 5: "God has promised to be with you wherever you go. Go in peace."
Session 6: "Go in the joy that God has given you."
Session 7: "May God's word of love be written in your hearts."
Session 8: "May God's word guide you with its shining light."
Closing Celebration: "May God's word be with you and your families."

Songs
THEME GATHERING SONG

I Have the Light of the Lord

Wanda Alger

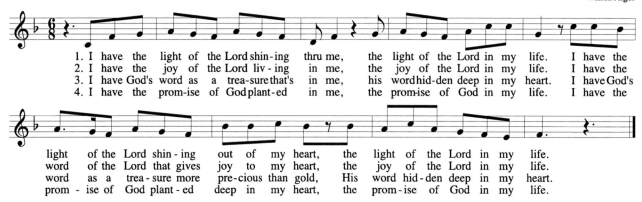

1. I have the light of the Lord shin-ing thru me, the light of the Lord in my life. I have the
2. I have the joy of the Lord liv-ing in me, the joy of the Lord in my life. I have the
3. I have God's word as a trea-sure that's in me, his word hid-den deep in my heart. I have God's
4. I have the prom-ise of God plant-ed in me, the prom-ise of God in my life. I have the

light of the Lord shin-ing out of my heart, the light of the Lord in my life.
word of the Lord that gives joy to my heart, the joy of the Lord in my life.
word as a trea-sure more pre-cious than gold, His word hid-den deep in my heart.
prom-ise of God plant-ed deep in my heart, the prom-ise of God in my life.

Copyright © 2000 by Wanda Alger. Used by permission.

Motions

Light: Touch fingers together on each hand, then touch fingertips together. Bring hands out, then spread fingers out to show a burst of light.

Joy: Use index fingers from both hands to trace a smiley face onto your face.

Word: Hold hands open like a book.

Promise: Hold right hand up at side, as if saying hello or promising an oath.

THEME SENDING SONG
We Are Marching (Siyahamba) (CCLI #4566559)
Text and music: South Africa. Arrangement copyright © 1984 by
    Utryck. Admin. by Walton Music Corporation.

KICK OFF SESSION
Genesis*
Text and music: Wes Hamm. Copyright © 2000 by Wes Hamm.

Ancient of Days (CCLI #798108)
Text and music: Jamie Harvill, Gary Sadler. Copyright © 1992
    Integrity's Hosanna! Music.

SESSION 1
Blessed Be Your Name (CCLI #3798438)
Text and music: Matt Redman. Copyright © 2002 Thankyou Music.
    Admin. by EMI Christian Music Publishing.

Ancient Words (CCLI #636947)
Text and music: Lynn DeShazo. Copyright © 2001 Integrity's
    Hosanna! Music.

SESSION 2
Jesus, Be the Center (Sing the Story #31)
Text and music: Michael Frye. Copyright © 1999 Vineyard Songs
    (UK/Eire). Admin. by Music Services.

New Testament Lullaby*
Text and music: Wes Hamm. Copyright © 2000 by Wes Hamm.

SESSION 3
I Can Hear Your Message
Text and music: Bryan Moyer Suderman. Copyright © 2009 by
    SmallTall Music.

He Has Made Me Glad (CCLI #1493)
Text and music: Leona Von Brethorst. Copyright © 1976 Maranatha
    Praise, Inc.

* Musical notation included on page 10

SESSION 4

The B-I-B-L-E
Text and music: Traditional.

Ancient Words (CCLI #636947)
Text and music: Lynn DeShazo. Copyright © 2001 Integrity's Hosanna!
    Music.

SESSION 5

I Am a Promise
Text and music: William J. and Gloria Gaither. Copyright © 1975
    William J. Gaither.

Obey My Voice
Text: Based on Jeremiah 7:23. Music: Sheilagh Nowacki. Copyright ©
    1972 by Sheilagh Nowacki.

SESSION 6

Hey, Hey Neighbor
Text and music: Roger Day. Copyright © 2000 by Roger Day.

SESSION 7

Give Me Joy in My Heart (change "Give me joy" to "Put
God's word")
Text and music: Traditional.

The Wise Man Built His House Upon the Rock
Text and music: Traditional.

SESSION 8

This Little Light of Mine (*Hymnal: A Worship Book* #401)
Text and music: African-American spiritual.

Thy Word (CCLI #14301)
Text and music: Michael W. Smith, Amy Grant. Copyright © 1984
    Meadowgreen Music.

We Are Marching (Siyahamba) (CCLI #4566559)
Text and music: South Africa. Arrangement copyright © 1984 by
    Utryck. Admin. by Walton Music Corporation.

CLOSING SESSION

We Are Marching (Siyahamba) (CCLI #4566559)
Text and music: South African. Arrangement copyright © 1984 by
    Utryck. Admin. by Walton Music Corporation.

GENERAL SONGS

Ancient of Days (CCLI #798108)
Text and music: Jamie Harvill, Gary Sadler. Copyright © 1992
    Integrity's Hosanna! Music.

Ancient Words (CCLI #636947)
Text and music: Lynn DeShazo. Copyright © 2001 Integrity's Hosanna!
    Music.

Blessed Be Your Name (CCLI #3798438)
Text and music: Matt Redman. Copyright © 2002 Thankyou Music.
    Admin. by EMI Christian Music Publishing.

Come, Now Is the Time to Worship (*Sing the Journey*
#9; CCLI #2430948)
Text and music: Brian Doerksen. Copyright © 1998 Vineyard Songs.

Days of Elijah (CCLI #1537904)
Text and music: Robin Mark. Copyright © 1997 Daybreak Music Ltd.

Give Me Joy in My Heart (change "Give me joy" to
"Put God's word")
Text and music: Traditional.

God Will Guide You
Text and music: Bryan Moyer Suderman. Copyright © 2009 SmallTall
    Music.

He Has Made Me Glad (CCLI #1493)
Text and music: Leona Von Brethorst. Copyright © 1976 Maranatha
    Praise, Inc.

Hey, Hey Neighbor
Text and music: Roger Day. Copyright © 2000 Roger Day.

Jesus, Be the Center (*Sing the Story* #31)
Text and music: Michael Frye. Copyright © 1999 Vineyard Songs
    (UK/Eire). Admin. by Music Services.

Kumbaya
Text and music: Traditional African melody.

The Lord Lift You Up (*Sing the Journey* #73)
Text and music: Patricia J. Shelly; arranged by Dennis Frisen-Carper.
    Copyright © 1983 by Patricia J. Shelley.

Obey My Voice
Text: Based on Jeremiah 7:23. Music: Sheilagh Nowacki. Copyright ©
    1972 by Sheilagh Nowacki.

Peace Before Us (*Sing the Story* #16)
Text: David Hass, based on a Navajo prayer. Music: David Haas.
    Copyright © 1987 GIA Publications, Inc.

This Little Light of Mine (*Hymnal: A Worship Book*
#401)
Text and music: African-American spiritual.

We Are Marching (Siyahamba) (CCLI #4566559)
Text and music: South African. Arrangement copyright © 1984 by
    Utryck. Admin. by Walton Music Corporation.

9

Genesis

Wes Hamm

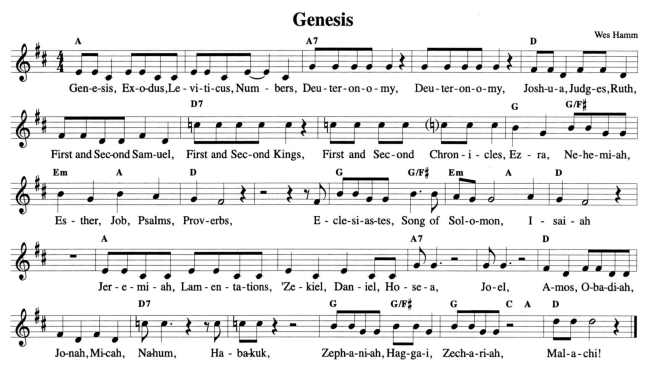

New Testament Lullaby

Wes Hamm

Bible memory verses & tips

Try to make Bible memory a part of the group's time together. Find time each session to practice the memory verses.

The overall goal is to memorize the books of the Old and New Testaments in order. This can be done through songs such as "Genesis" (page 10) and "New Testament Lullaby" (page 10). Send a copy of the books of the Bible home with the children, and encourage them to learn it between meeting times.

Choose a time to practice the memory text: during the meal or snack, during gathering time, before the Bible story, during craft time, or as part of the sending.

Pair children with a memory mentor to help them learn the text together.

The following are two Bible memory options:

I. Books of the Bible

Old Testament		New Testament
Genesis	Amos	Matthew
Exodus	Obadiah	Mark
Leviticus	Jonah	Luke
Numbers	Micah	John
Deuteronomy	Nahum	Acts of the Apostles
Joshua	Habakkuk	Romans
Judges	Zephaniah	1 Corinthians
Ruth	Haggai	2 Corinthians
1 Samuel	Zechariah	Galatians
2 Samuel	Malachi	Ephesians
1 Kings		Philippians
2 Kings		Colossians
1 Chronicles		1 Thessalonians
2 Chronicles		2 Thessalonians
Ezra		1 Timothy
Nehemiah		2 Timothy
Esther		Titus
Job		Philemon
Psalms		Hebrews
Proverbs		James
Ecclesiastes		1 Peter
Song of Solomon		2 Peter
Isaiah		1 John
Jeremiah		2 John
Lamentations		3 John
Ezekiel		Jude
Daniel		Revelation
Hosea		
Joel		

2. Selected Verses

Learn some or all of these verses over the course of the program.

Kick off session: I treasure your word in my heart, so that I may not sin against you. Psalm 119:11

Session 1: The law of the LORD is perfect, reviving the soul; the decrees of the Lord are sure, making wise the simple. Psalm 19:7

Session 2: I delight to do your will, O my God; your law is within my heart. Psalm 40:8

Session 3: Happy are those whose way is blameless, who walk in the law of the LORD. Psalm 119:1

Session 4: How can young people keep their way pure? By guarding it according to your word. Psalm 119:9

Session 5: The promises of the Lord are the promises that are pure. Psalm 12:6a

Session 6: You shall love the Lord your God with all your heart, and with all your soul, and with all your strength, and with all your mind; and your neighbor as yourself. Luke 10:27

Session 7: With my whole heart I seek you; do not let me stray from your commandments. Psalm 119:10

Session 8: Your word is a lamp to my feet and a light to my path. Psalm 119:105

Note
. . . .
Feel free to use a different Bible translation if you prefer.

FUN WAYS TO MEMORIZE SCRIPTURE:

1. **Play a game using flash cards.** Use one card for each word. Distribute the cards to the children. Ask them to line up holding their cards in the proper order.

2. **Place the flash cards on a wall.** Children remove one word at a time and repeat the entire verse until all the cards are gone.

3. **Create hand motions to key words.**

4. **Say the verse while doing different actions** (running in place, hopping on one foot, stride jumps, marching).

5. **Stand or sit in a circle,** and assign phrases or words for each child or small group to repeat. Continue until everyone knows the verse.

6. **Balloon tap:** Children tap a balloon in the air each time they say a word in the verse.

7. **Ball throw:** Invite the children to throw a ball to each other as they say the next word in the verse.

8. **Use rhythm instruments and chant the text.**

9. **Invite children to illustrate key words** and use the pictures as memory aids.

10. **Repeat the memory text often in a variety of settings.** Do it while the children eat, when they gather, while they work on a craft or play a game, or at the end of the session.

Book list

Set up a mini-library with children's Bible books and other books about the Bible. Check with your church, school, or public librarian for these and other books.

1. Backhouse, Robert. *The Student Guide to Bible People*. Minneapolis: Augsburg, 1996.
2. Doney, Meryl. *How the Bible Came to Us: The Story of the Book That Changed the World*. Colorado Springs: Lion Publishing, 1985.
3. Hall, Terry. *Bible Almanac for Kids*. Lakeland, FL: White Stone Books, 2004.
4. Motyer, Dr. Stephen. *Who's Who in the Bible: An Illustrated Guide*. New York: DK Publishing, 1998.
5. Meyer, Mary Clemens. *Walking with Jesus: Stories about real people who return good for evil*. Scottdale, PA: Herald Press, 1992.
6. *My Bible Reading Chart*. Scottdale, PA: Faith & Life Resources, 2006.
7. Osborne, Rick, and K. Christi Bowler. *I Want to Know About the Bible*. Grand Rapids, MI: Zondervan, 1998.
8. Palacco, Patricia. *The Bee Tree*. New York: Puffin Books, 1998.
9. Rock, Lois. *The Time of Jesus: Crafts to Make*. Colorado Springs: Lion Publishing, 1998.
10. Seiling, Rebecca. *Plant a Seed of Peace*. Scottdale, PA: Herald Press, 2007.
11. Sasso, Sandy Eisenberg. *God's Paintbrush*. Woodstock, VT: Jewish Lights Publishing, 1992.

RECOMMENDED BOOKS FOR EACH SESSION
Kickoff
1. Anderson, Joel. *Jonah's Trash . . . God's Treasure*. Nashville, TN: Thomas Nelson, 1998.

Session 1
1. Cooper, Ilene. *The Dead Sea Scrolls*. New York: HarperCollins, 1997.
2. Palacco, Patricia. *The Bee Tree*. New York: Puffin Books, 1998.

Session 2
1. DePaola, Tomie. *The Parables of Jesus*. New York: Holiday House, 1987.

Session 3
1. Seiling, Rebecca. *Plant a Seed of Peace*. "The Secret Church Grows." Scottdale, PA: Herald Press, 2007.
2. Martin Jr., Bill, and Michael Sampson. *Adam, Adam, What Do You See?* Nashville, TN: Thomas Nelson, Inc., 2000.

Session 4
1. Polacco, Patricia. *The Keeping Quilt*. New York: Simon & Schuster, 1988.

Session 5
1. Countryman, Jack, and Terri Gibbs. *God's Promises for Kids*. Nashville, TN: Thomas Nelson, 2003.
2. Munsch, Robert. *A Promise is a Promise*. Willowdale, ON: Firefly Books, 1988.

Session 6
1. Palmer, Glenda. *Good Sam: Jesus' Story of the Good Samaritan.* Cincinnati, OH: Standard Publishing, 1996.

Session 7
1. Fox, Mem. *Koala Lou.* New York: Voyager Books, 1988.

Session 8
1. Lewis, E. B., illustrator. *This Little Light of Mine.* New York: Simon and Schuster Books for Young Readers, 2005.

Closing
1. Rouss, Sylvia A. *Sammy Spider's First Simchat Torah.* Minneapolis: Kar-Ben Publishing, 2010.

Snacks

Suggestions are given for general snacks and for specific snacks to use in various sessions. If you begin with a meal, serve foods from the global community. Use your favorite recipes or choose recipes from *Extending the Table: A World Community Cookbook* by Joetta Handrich Schlabach (Scottdale, PA: Herald Press, 1991). Be aware of food allergies. It is best not to use nuts or nut products.

If you want the children to make snacks as part of their activities, you will find simple recipes in these cookbooks:
1. Lind, Mary Beth, and Cathleen Hockman-Wert. *Simply in Season.* Scottdale, PA: Herald Press, 2009.
2. Beach, Mark, and Julie Kauffman. *Simply in Season for Children.* Scottdale, PA: Herald Press, 2006.
3. Longacre, Doris Janzen. *More-with-Less Cookbook.* Scottdale, PA: Herald Press, 1976.

General snack ideas
- animal crackers and apples cut in half (revealing the seeds)
- pretzels in different shapes, sizes, and flavors
- popcorn with different flavorings
- vegetables such as cucumbers, carrot and celery sticks, pepper rings, broccoli, cherry tomatoes variety of low-calorie dips
- crackers and cheese slices or cheese spread
- fresh fruit kabobs with apples, oranges, melons, berries, interspersed with mini marshmallows for variety; supply wooden skewers and have the children make their own kebob; add a yogurt dip
- nutritious cookies and squares
- cupcakes

KICKOFF SESSION
Serve a treasure mix of raisins, chocolate chips, dried cranberries, dried apricots, cereal, marshmallows, pretzels, and other items.

SESSION 1
Make edible Bible scrolls (page 27, a Kids Create activity).

SESSION 2
Make bear paw cookies to symbolize feet walking with Jesus. Use cookies shaped like feet.

SESSION 3
Make popcorn balls to eat and to share with others.

SESSION 4
Make Bible brownies (page 50, a Kids Create activity).

SESSION 5
Make date treats by rolling moist, pitted, freshly chopped dates in flaked coconut. Top with an almond.

SESSION 6
Serve an assortment of pita bread, olives, dried apricots, dried figs, hummus, and flatbread crackers.

SESSION 7
Make heart snacks. Use cereal or pretzel letters to create Bible words. Use frosting to attach words to heart-shaped sugar cookies.

SESSION 8
Serve yellow or orange jellied treats to symbolize light.

CLOSING CELEBRATION
Options: Enjoy treats such as ice cream sundaes with toppings, or cupcakes and juice. Have a campfire roast with hotdogs and marshmallows.

Extended craft projects

Each session includes a variety of craft ideas. Some children, especially older ones, enjoy working on a larger project that extends over a number of weeks. Instead of choosing a craft for each session, you may wish to choose a craft that extends for several sessions.

TREASURE CHEST

The Bible is full of treasured verses. Children will make a treasure box to hold their memory verses.

Materials: wooden boxes or shoe boxes, paints, paint brushes, adhesive gems or sequins, markers, index cards, pens

- Children will decorate their treasure chests with craft supplies.
- Additional decorations may be added each week.
- Children will write their memory verse for each session onto an index card, decorate it, and add it to the treasure chest.

BIBLE WALL HANGING

The Bible contains many wonderful stories. Children will make a wall hanging to remind them of favorite stories in the Bible.

Materials: heavy canvas fabric (white or beige), wooden dowel, pencils, fabric paints or markers, fine permanent marker, paintbrushes

- Prepare fabric ahead of time. Cut a piece of heavy canvas fabric about 12 by 14 in. /30 by 35 cm. On the 14-in. /35-cm side, fold the material down 2 in. / 5 cm, and sew to make a sleeve for a wooden dowel to slip through.
- Use a pencil to make two crossing, faint lines to divide the space into four equal squares. These will be the areas in which children will create pictures of their favorite Bible stories.
- Children can plan their drawing by lightly drawing in pencil before using fabric paints or markers. If they wish to include favorite Bible verses, these can be printed on the fabric with a fine permanent marker.

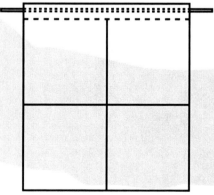

- Children may also want to write on their wall hangings using calligraphy. See page 17 for a complete calligraphy alphabet.

A A B B C C D D E F F F

G H I J K K L L M N O

P Q 2 R R S T T U V

W X X Y Z Z

a b c d c l d e f f g h i j k l m n

o f p p q a r s t t u v w x x y z

1 2 3 4 5 6 7 8 9 ∝ &

Tips on managing unwanted behavior

- **Be prepared.** Give yourself time to read through the session and prepare. Be in the meeting area early so you are ready to greet children as they arrive. The session actually begins the minute the first child arrives.

- **Be consistent.** Create, display, and review guidelines for how the group behaves together, and remind children often of expectations. Stop the session and address unwanted behavior as often as necessary so children know you are serious about expectations.

- **Be observant.** Observe the different abilities and interests of each child. Keep the session active. Engage children's minds and bodies as you teach. As often as possible, let children move around. For example, use actions with songs and memory work, sit on the floor for the Bible story, and stand at a table for crafts.

- **Be encouraging.** Reinforce positive behaviors in affirming, spoken ways. Wait until everyone is quiet and attentive before beginning instructions. Speak clearly and slowly, making sure everyone understands what is being said.

- **Be ready to apologize.** If you have made a mistake, apologize to the child or the group. This can be a teachable moment as you model what it means to be a peacemaker.

- **Be a leader, not a buddy.** Let children know you care about them, but relate to them as a leader. Children respect you more when they know what to expect from you.

- **Seek help from others.** Ask an adult to give extra attention to any child with behavioral challenges. Seek counsel from other leaders and parents. If you do not know how to handle a discipline challenge, talk to someone who can help you.

- **Pray.** Pray that each child may experience God's love and peace, especially while in your care.

- **Choose to love each child unconditionally** regardless of his or her behavior.

- **Practice peacemaking** and conflict resolution skills at all times.

Kickoff Session
Full of treasures

(kick off)

• •

Use this session to introduce children to the overall theme of discovering the Bible. Children like to imagine finding a treasure, and sometimes even dig in search of one. The Bible is filled with stories about the people of Israel and Jesus and his followers; it is filled with treasures that help us follow God's way. Children of all ages can learn to treasure the Bible.

BIBLE TEXT
Matthew 6:21

FAITH CHALLENGE
We treasure the Bible.

ADVANCE PREPARATION
- Read through the entire session, and decide what you will do.
- Set up the room/space for the various activities.
- Gather props for the story: Bible, large treasure chest.
- Gather supplies for the activities you choose to do.
- Prepare a snack (see p. 14).

Kids Cluster

1. **Plan an activity for the early arrivals.** Check page 6 for ideas.
2. **If the children do not know each other,** make name tags and play some get-acquainted games (p. 6).
3. **Welcome the children,** and gather for a time of singing (p. 8). Be sure to include action songs, familiar songs, favorite songs, and new songs.

Kids Dig the Bible

Story tip

Act this story out as you tell it. Use your treasure chest. Pretend to find the chest and then bury it. Alternatively, ask a child to act it out as you tell it. Make the biblical story come alive.

1. **Begin with the theme song,** "I Have the Light of the Lord" (p. 8). Pray a simple prayer.
2. **Introduce the theme of the day:** We treasure the Bible.
3. **Open a large treasure chest to find a Bible.**
4. **Open the Bible to Matthew 6:21.** Show the children where today's story can be found. Read this story:

Jesus told this story: The kingdom of God is like a treasure that is hidden in a field. One day a man walked by the field and found the treasure. He was so excited that he jumped for joy. He couldn't believe what he found. What a miracle! Then the man buried the treasure and left to find the owner of the land. He sold everything he owned to buy the field. He knew that this treasure was more precious than anything else in the whole world.

Tip

Use these questions/ideas as conversation points during the craft time. It is not necessary to sit quietly and reflect on these points, but do include them during other activities.

5. **Talk about the Bible**
   - What is the treasure that was hidden in the field?
   - What would this treasure look like?
   - Who might be excited about finding this type of treasure? Why?
   - Imagine finding a treasure in a field. What would you give up in order to keep that treasure?
   - Think about the things in your house. What do you treasure most?
   - Who do you treasure?
   - How is the Bible like a precious treasure?
   - What treasures have you already found in the Bible?

6. **Read Proverbs 2:1-6 aloud.** Talk about wisdom as the greatest treasure we can find in God's word, the Bible.

Fun fact

Many people have treasured the Bible over the years. It is the world's best-selling and most widely distributed book. Between 1815 and 1975, 2.5 billion copies of the Bible were distributed.

7. **Work on memorizing the books of the Bible in order** (p. 11). There are many songs that can be found online to help children learn, like "Genesis" and "New Testament Lullaby." Learn the books at a pace that the group can handle.

Many of the selected verses for Bible memory come from the book of Psalms. Introduce the book of Psalms. Explain that psalms are poems and songs written to and about God, God's way and God's love. Psalms were read or sung out loud, and they tell us about people feeling deep joy and sorrow, happiness and sadness.

Memory tip

Send home a decorated paper that lists the books of the Old and New Testaments in order. Children can practice memorizing at home.

Recite together Psalm 119:11: "I treasure your word in my heart, so that I may not sin against you." Use Bible memory ideas that are found on page 12. *Note:* Psalm 119 is the longest chapter in the Bible. The writer declares his great love for God's word in 176 verses.

8. **If time permits, tell or read the story** "A Bible That Keeps on Working" (p. 23). This could be done as the children are working or eating a snack.

Kids Create

TREASURE CHEST
(INDIVIDUAL)
Children will make a treasure box to hold their memory verses from each session. Treasure chests can be made from shoe boxes or wooden boxes purchased at dollar or craft stores. See "Extended craft projects" on page 16 for more details.

TIP
Type out the Bible memory verse ahead of time, and have children glue the verse to an index card. They can draw pictures to decorate their card before placing it into the treasure chest.

TIP
Chests can be kept in the room for children to continue to decorate. One memory verse can be added each session.

TREASURE PICTURE FRAMES
(INDIVIDUAL)
One thing we learn in the Bible is that we are God's special treasures.

Materials: small wooden picture frames, acrylic paints, paintbrushes, adhesive gems
Guide the children in doing the following:
- Think about ways they are special treasures and decorate their picture frame accordingly.
- Label the frame "God's treasure!"

TIP
Take digital pictures of the children who make this craft, and bring the printed photos to the next session. These photos can be placed in the frame that they decorated.

TRASH TO TREASURE
(INDIVIDUAL)
Children will create treasures made from items destined for the landfill or recycling depots.

Materials: white glue, scissors, magnets with adhesive backing, markers, plastic containers, small glass jars, boxboard or poster board, scraps of fabric, scraps of ribbon, scraps of paper, and other items
- Ideas for treasures include magnets, decorated containers, plant pots, and posters.

BIBLE ACROSTIC
(GROUP)
Psalm 119 was written as an acrostic poem. Each section of the poem starts with the next letter in the Hebrew alphabet. Children will work together to write an acrostic poem about the Bible, using the English alphabet. This activity can also gauge how much your group knows already about the Bible.

Materials: easel paper, markers
Guide the children in doing the following:
- Starting with A, list the letters of the alphabet in order down the left-hand side of the page.
- Suggest lines of the poem that will begin with the corresponding letter of the alphabet. Lines in the poem can be just one word or whole phrases.

Kids Move

TREASURE HUNT
(GROUP)

We can find many treasures in the Bible. In this game, children will practice looking up biblical references to find hidden clues.

Materials: photocopy of treasure hunt clues listed below and on page 23, Bibles, special snack/reward for a prize

- Ahead of time, adapt and prepare the clue hiding places to suit your surroundings. Hide each clue in the following areas:

  Clue 1: given to the group at the beginning of the hunt
  Clue 2: hidden at main entrance (gates) of the building
  Clue 3: hidden in pastor's study or office
  Clue 4: hidden in church mailboxes (letters)
  Clue 5: hidden near drinking fountain
  Clue 6: hidden in sanctuary
  Clue 7: hidden in library
  Clue 8: hidden in kitchen
  Clue 9: hidden in nursery
  Clue 10: hidden in pulpit
  Clue 11: hidden near offering plates

Guide the children in doing the following:
- Work together in one or two groups. An adult may help each group find the references in the Bible.
- At each hiding place, there will be a biblical reference to find. Figure out the corresponding place in the building where the next clue will be found.

Offer the children a special snack or prize at the end of the hunt.

Closing
For closing ideas, see page 7.

TREASURE, TREASURE SO HIGH
(GROUP)

Children will hunt for small treasures hidden around the room.

Materials: coin
- The child who is IT hides a coin while the other players close their eyes.
- When the coin is hidden, IT says, "Treasure, treasure, so high!" and indicates on his or her body the height of the hiding place.
- Players walk up to IT, copy the measurement, and walk around the room, looking for the coin at that height.
- The person who finds the coin is IT during the next round.

PRUI
(GROUP)

This game is fun for children because there is a hidden "Prui." The goal is to find the Prui and join together with her or him.
- Everyone closes their eyes, and a leader chooses the Prui with a quiet tap on the shoulder.
- Prui may open his or her eyes, but the other players keep eyes closed.
- Players begin wandering around the room. When they bump into someone, they shake hands, then ask, "Prui?" If the other person answers, "Prui?" they both keep on searching.
- Prui cannot speak, so when someone shakes Prui's hand, Prui does not respond. When someone finds the Prui, she or he becomes part of the Prui by joining hands.
- If several people have already joined with the Prui, the new joiner must find the end of the chain and join there. If players bump into the middle of the Prui chain, they must find their way to the end of the Prui to shake hands.
- When the last player joins the chain, all let out a cheer.

TREASURE HUNT CLUES RESOURCE

Clue 1. Read Psalm 122:1. Go to the main place people enter your church.

Clue 2. This is what Ezra did in Ezra 7:10. Go to the place where your pastor does this.

Clue 3. In 2 Thessalonians 3:17, Paul talks about writing a _____. Where would you go to receive these at church?

Clue 4. Read Proverbs 18:4. Go to the place that is described here.

Clue 5. In Exodus 25:8, God told Moses to make this. Go to the front of this.

Clue 6. What did King Jehoiakim burn in Jeremiah 36:20-24? Go to the church room where we store these in their modern form.

Clue 7. Read Genesis 25:34. Jacob gave Esau _____ in exchange for his birthright as the oldest son. Go to the place in the church where this could be made.

Clue 8. Read Exodus 2:3. Go to the special room in the church for those the age of the child described in this verse.

Clue 9. What did Paul do in Acts 9:20? Go to the place where people do this during worship.

Clue 10. Find the containers used to collect what is described in Luke 21:1-2.

"A BIBLE THAT KEEPS ON WORKING"

If Bibles could talk, they would have wonderful adventures to tell. This is the story of a Bible that belonged to David Hostetler, a missionary in Brazil. The Bible was written in Portuguese, the language people speak in Brazil. David enjoyed his new Bible. It had a beautiful black leather cover. He used his Bible a lot.

After fourteen years, the Hostetler family moved back to the United States. David said, "This Bible is getting old. I have other Bibles. I'll leave this Bible in Brazil."

The Schwartzentruber family moved into the house where the Hostetlers had lived. One day the father, Kenneth, found a book that had turned green with mold. It was in a box that had been left in the garage. (During the rainy season in Brazil, lots of things turn green with mold, because it is so damp.) It was David's old leather Bible. Kenneth cleaned it, polished the cover with black shoe polish, and began to use it.

Kenneth enjoyed this old Bible that he had rescued from the mold. He used the Bible for twenty-five years. He underlined verses that were important to him. When it was time to move back to Canada, Kenneth wondered, "What should I do with my old Bible? It's falling apart."

Kenneth gave the old Bible to his friend Antonio. "Would you keep this Bible for me? I have used it for a long time and marked a lot of verses."

A few years ago, Antonio wrote to Kenneth. "Your old Bible is still working!" said Antonio. "I left it in my truck. My daughter, Silvia, started reading it! Silvia did not want to learn about Jesus before she started reading this old Bible. Maybe it will help her decide to love and follow Jesus." Kenneth prays for Silvia as she uses his old Bible. He prays for people in Brazil buying new Bibles. He prays for thousands of children in Brazil receiving children's Bibles. He hopes that each Bible will help people learn to know and follow God.

Session 1
Rolls of scrolls

(1)

The story of the Bible's history is fascinating. Stories were passed on from one generation to the next and then painstakingly copied by scribes onto scrolls. This session introduces children to the making of the Old Testament.

BIBLE TEXT
2 Kings 22:1-13; 23:1-3

FAITH CHALLENGE
We discover the Old Testament.

ADVANCE PREPARATION
- Read through the entire session, and decide what you will do.
- Set up the room/space for the various activities.
- Gather supplies for the activities you choose to do.
- Prepare a snack (p. 14).

Kids Cluster

1. **Plan an activity for the early arrivals.** Check page 6 for ideas.
2. **If the children do not know each other,** make name tags and play some ice-breaker games (p. 6).
3. **Welcome the children, and gather for a time of singing** (p. 8). Be sure to include action songs, familiar songs, favorite songs, and new songs.

Kids Dig the Bible

Tip · · · · · · · · · ·

If there are those who like to act, consider handing out parts ahead of time to "King Josiah Chooses to Obey God" from *Fun Bible Skits 3* by David M. Morrow (Scottdale, PA: Faith and Life Resources, 2007).

Tip · · · · · · · · · ·

Use these questions/ideas as conversation points during the craft time. It is not necessary to sit quietly and reflect on these points, but do include them during other activities.

Tip · · · · · · · · · ·

Some people use the terms "Hebrew Scriptures" or "Hebrew Bible" instead of "Old Testament." "Old Testament" is the Christian name for this material.

Fun Fact · · · · · · · ·

Scrolls were often stored in clay jars for safe keeping.

Memory tip · · · · · ·

Make an index card with today's memory verse for children to put in their treasure chests made last session. Children can continue to decorate their chests as an optional activity.

1. **Begin with the theme song,** "I Have the Light of the Lord" (p. 8), or a simple prayer.

2. **Introduce the theme of the day:** We discover the Old Testament.

3. **Show where 2 Kings can be found in your Bible.** Read this Bible story based on 2 Kings 22:1-13; 23:1-3.

Josiah was eight years old when he became king. What an important job for a young boy! Josiah wanted to worship God. He decided to hire carpenters and builders to repair the temple.

During the repairs, the priest found a treasure in the temple.

He shouted with joy, "I have found the Book of the Law in the temple of the Lord! Go tell the king!"

King Josiah was so excited that the priest had found a long-lost scroll of God's laws. What a wonderful treasure! But when the king heard the scroll being read, he said, "The people have not been following God's teaching. Something must change."

King Josiah called all the people together. They gathered at the temple. The king read the words in the Book of the Law so that everyone could hear them. Then King Josiah promised to love and worship God with all his heart and soul. And all the people made the same promise.

4. **Talk about the Bible**
   - I wonder why King Josiah was so excited about finding and reading these scrolls.
   - Imagine being excited to open the Bible and read a story.
   - King Josiah was a young king who treasured God's word. How can we show that we treasure the Bible today?
   - Hearing the scroll read out loud caused the people to change. What story have you heard that made you change your behavior in some way?

5. **Talk about the Book of the Law,** which may have referred to Deuteronomy. Deuteronomy is one of the first five books in the Bible and is in a section called the Books of the Law, the Torah, or the Pentateuch ("five books"). This group of writings includes Genesis, Exodus, Leviticus, Numbers, and Deuteronomy. These five books were written onto one scroll.

6. **Continue to learn the books of the Bible in order.** Listen to the song "Genesis" (p. 10) to recite the books of the Old Testament together.

Recite together Psalm 19:7: "The law of the LORD is perfect, reviving the soul; the decrees of the LORD are sure, making wise the simple." Use ideas from page 12 to aid in Bible memory.

7. **Briefly tell about a young shepherd boy's exciting discovery** of the Dead Sea Scrolls in 1947. Read "Writings Hidden in a Cave" (p. 30). People all over the world were excited about this discovery. Archaeologists studied these scrolls and found they were very close to what the scribes had copied thousands of years before. This young shepherd boy had made a wonderful discovery.

Kids Create

BISCUIT BIBLE SCROLLS
(SMALL GROUP)
Materials: canned biscuits or croissants, butter, cinnamon sugar, pretzel sticks, baking sheet

Divide the children into small groups for this activity, each group with adult supervision, then guide the children in the following:
- Flatten a biscuit to make a long, thin rectangle.
- Spread with a small amount of butter, and sprinkle with cinnamon sugar. This can represent the sweetness of the words in the Bible.
- Place a pretzel stick at each end, and roll toward the center. Bake according to directions on the biscuit can.

TIP
While you make and eat these, tell the story of God telling Ezekiel to eat a scroll. Ezekiel ate the scroll and thought it tasted as sweet as honey. This can be found in Ezekiel 3:1-3.

MAKE A SCROLL
(INDIVIDUAL)
Materials: long piece of paper, dowel rods or wooden chopsticks, tape or glue, ribbon

Guide the children in the following:
- Tape or glue wooden sticks to the ends of the paper.
- Roll to form a scroll, and tie a ribbon around it.
- The Old Testament was written in Hebrew. On the scrolls, practice writing in Hebrew by looking at the Hebrew alphabet on page 31.
- Write this session's memory verse in the scroll.

Optional: Make tiny scrolls out of paper and toothpicks. Use self-hardening clay to make pots to store them.

PHYLACTERIES
(INDIVIDUAL)

Children will make phylacteries (pockets) containing God's laws. The Hebrew people believed that God had given them important laws to follow. They wore small black leather boxes containing words from the Torah (first five books of the Bible) strapped to their upper left arm or above their forehead.

Materials: a piece of soft black leather, vinyl, or felt 6 by 6 in. / 15 by 15 cm; a thick needle; heavy thread; metal skewer; a thick polystyrene block; paper; pen; ink

Guide the children in the following (adults will need to supervise this activity):

- Cut the piece of leather as shown in the illustration.
- Place the upper piece in the center of the lower piece. Stitch with heavy thread, using a blanket stitch. Leave one short side open.
- Cut a piece of paper small enough to slip into the pocket.
- Copy a verse from the Old Testament onto the paper (particularly from the Torah).
- Roll the paper into a tight bundle, and tie it with thread. Place it inside the pocket.
- Stitch the opening shut, and stitch a second time around.
- Lay the pocket on a polystyrene block, and make a hole with a skewer.
- Thread three long pieces of thread through the hole. Braid each side of three threads into a cord, and knot the end. Tie the pocket onto forehead or arm.

Tip . . . .
Scribes followed special rules. Each letter and word was counted and compared with the original text. A page with more than three mistakes was thrown out. A scribe wiped his pen before writing God's name. A scribe did not write one word from memory but said each word before writing it.

COPYCAT SCRIBES
(INDIVIDUAL)

Scribes had very important jobs in the ancient world. There were no photocopiers back then! The scribe's skills were valued because he could write. Few people could read or write at that time. One of the scribe's jobs was to copy manuscripts very carefully, making no mistakes. Scribes wrote with ink on either papyrus, a paper made from stems of a reed plant, or vellum, animal skins that had been cleaned and treated. It was a lot of work to make papyrus paper or vellum, so scribes were careful to do their best work when writing.

Materials: paper, markers, colored pencils, pens, calligraphy markers (optional)
Guide the children in the following:
- Choose a memory text from this series to copy several times.
- Use markers to try to print in a calligraphy style (see p. 31).
Encourage children to take their time and do their best work, pretending to be scribes in Bible times.

28

Kids Move

HIDE AND SEEK
(GROUP)
The priest found a hidden scroll, and King Josiah rejoiced. Many years later, a shepherd boy found the Dead Sea scrolls in a cave. This caused much rejoicing as well. Hide and seek can be played in a couple of ways.

- A scroll can be hidden and the group needs to find it.
- A child could play the role of the shepherd boy while the rest of the group hides and pretends to be the hidden Dead Sea scrolls.

CARRY GOD'S MESSAGE
(GROUP)
This game is played like "Steal the bacon."

Materials: an object to represent the "message"
Guide the children in the following:
- Form two lines of players, and number the players on each team.
- The leader places the "message" midway between the lines, and calls out numbers at random.
- The players whose number is called must try to take the "message" and return to their lines without being tagged by the other.
- A player may not be tagged if she or he is not holding the message.
- Successfully delivering the "message" gives the team a point.
- Renumber the teams occasionally so that players face different opponents.

JOSIAH SAYS
(GROUP)
After hearing the scroll read aloud, King Josiah and the people decided to follow God's ways. King Josiah was a good leader in that he led his people to honor God.
Guide the children in the following:
- One child plays King Josiah, directing the others in actions, just like the game "Simon Says."
- When King Josiah says, "King Josiah says jump in place (or another action)," follow the action.
- If King Josiah simply says, "Jump in place," do not follow the action.
- Children who do the actions that are not preceded by "King Josiah says" are out of the game.
- Play until only one child is left, and he or she is the new King Josiah.

MIRROR GAME
(PARTNERS)
Scribes worked to copy the Old Testament writings word for word over and over again. They had to copy exactly what was on the page.
Guide the children in the following:
- Partner A moves slowly, facing Partner B.
- Partner B copies every move Partner A makes.
- Switch roles.

Closing
For closing ideas, see page 7.

"WRITINGS HIDDEN IN A CAVE"
FROM "THE BIBLE: GOD'S GOOD NEWS"
by Phyllis Martens. (*Come and See* Herald Press Bible School Series, 1989).

One day a Bedouin shepherd boy was wandering through the bare hills near the Dead Sea, looking for a lost goat. The steep sides of the hills were full of caves. The boy threw a stone into a cave and heard something break. The shepherds found the stone had hit an earthen jar in which a scroll had been stored. In the caves, they found more writings in jars.

One book, Isaiah, was made of 17 leather sheets sewed together to make a roll 24 ft. / 7 m long. There were copies of every Old Testament book except Esther. These became known as the Dead Sea Scrolls. Until then, the oldest copies of the Hebrew scriptures (Old Testament books) available were made in the ninth century. The 2,000-year-old Dead Sea Scrolls were made 1,000 years earlier! Yet scholars found very little difference between the early and later copies. The scribes had been very careful all those hundreds of years.

Session 2
Walking with Jesus

This session introduces children to the New Testament. This section of the Bible contains stories and letters about Jesus, his death, and his resurrection. Jesus went to various synagogues, teaching and reading from Old Testament scrolls. Scripture was very important to Jesus. Today's story includes Jesus reading from the scroll of Isaiah as he announces his ministry to his home community in the temple.

BIBLE TEXT
Luke 4:16-21

FAITH CHALLENGE
We discover the New Testament.

ADVANCE PREPARATION
- Read through the entire session, and decide what you will do.
- Set up the room/space for the various activities.
- Gather storytelling props: bathrobe, scroll.
- Gather supplies for the craft or game you choose.
- Prepare a snack (p. 14).

Kids Cluster

1. **Plan an activity for the early arrivals.** Check page 6 for ideas.
2. **Welcome the children, and gather for a time of singing** (p. 8). Be sure to include action songs, familiar songs, favorite songs, and new songs.

Kids Dig the Bible

1. **Begin with the theme song,** "I Have the Light of the Lord" (p. 8), or a simple prayer.

2. **Introduce the theme of the day:** We discover the New Testament.

3. **Today's Bible text comes from the New Testament,** which tells the story of Jesus' life, teachings, death, and resurrection. The New Testament Gospels and letters were written almost two thousand years ago. The New Testament was written after the Old Testament, but they are both considered ancient texts. Jesus heard and read the Old Testament scrolls in the temple as he was growing up. Scripture was very important to him.

4. **Open your Bible to Luke 4,** and show the children where today's story comes from. Have two volunteers act out today's story, based on Luke 4:16-21. One child can play the role of Jesus when he was a young man. Provide a bathrobe for a costume and a scroll. The other child can be the narrator.

   Narrator: Jesus grew up in a small town named Nazareth. When Jesus was about thirty years old, he began to travel around the region of Galilee to preach, teach, and heal the sick. Jesus was filled with the power of the Spirit. People began talking about Jesus, praising the man who taught in their synagogues.

   One Sabbath, Jesus returned to Nazareth, his hometown. As he always did on the Sabbath, he went to the synagogue for worship. He was handed the scroll of the prophet Isaiah. Unrolling the scroll, he stood up and began reading.

   Jesus: God's Spirit is on me. God has chosen me to bring good news to the poor. God has sent me to announce pardon to prisoners and recovery of sight to the blind, to set people free, to proclaim the year of the Lord's favor.

Tip . . . .
Use these questions/ ideas as conversation points during the craft time. It is not necessary to sit quietly and reflect on these points, but do include them during other activities.

5. **Talk about the Bible**
   - I wonder why Jesus read from the Isaiah scroll.
   - Why did Jesus choose those verses to read aloud?
   - Chapters and verses were not marked in the scroll. I wonder how Jesus found these words in Isaiah. He must have known his scriptures well.
   - What did the crowd think as he did that?
   - I wonder what things Jesus told people as he taught in other synagogues.
   - Jesus' message is about good news. How can we share this good news with others?
   - I wonder what other good news can be found in the Bible.

6. **Sing "Genesis"** (p. 10) to recite the books of the Old Testament in order. Sing "New Testament Lullaby" (p. 10) to recite the books of the New Testament.

Practice today's memory verse, Psalm 40:8: "I delight to do your will, O my God; your law is within my heart." Look on page 12 for creative Bible memorization ideas.

Kids Create

BIBLE BOOKS POSTER
(INDIVIDUAL OR GROUP)

Materials: labels with Old Testament and New Testament book names printed on them, construction paper, pencils

Ahead of time, type or print out the sixty-six books of the Bible onto label stickers, then **guide the children in the following:**
- Put the stickers onto a long strip of construction paper in order.
- Write a line to divide the Old Testament from the New Testament.

LETTER POUCH
(INDIVIDUAL)

Letters from the New Testament were very important to the early churches. These letters were read aloud, saved, read again, and eventually copied and made into a collection of stories and letters that became the New Testament. Children will make a letter pouch to keep important letters and cards that they would like to read again.

TIP
Early Christian churches circulated letters written by Paul. They wrote stories of Jesus' life, death, and resurrection.

Materials: fabric or poster board, threaded needles or stapler, adhesive circles, fabric markers or markers

Guide the children in the following:
- Following the template (p. 37), cut out a piece of fabric or poster board.
- For fabric pouches, stitch the sides shut. For poster board pouches, staple the sides.
- Put an adhesive circle on the flap to close the pouch.
- Decorate the pouch with fabric markers, markers, or other craft items. A favorite Bible memory verse can be printed on the outside as well.

GOOD NEWSPAPER
(SMALL GROUP)

Often we read bad news in the newspapers. Jesus announced good news, and we are to do the same. Children will make a giant newspaper front page that highlights good news in the world.

Materials: easel paper, markers, denominational newspapers or magazines, scissors, glue sticks

Guide the children in the following:
- On a sheet of easel paper, write your own headlines or stories. Include hopeful pictures or photos.
- Search through denominational periodicals for headlines of good news. Cut and paste them to the easel paper.

CODEX
(INDIVIDUAL)

Some scrolls were 30 ft. / 9 m long! It was difficult for people to roll and unroll the heavy scrolls, so they began to pile sheets of papyrus on top of each other, fold them, and bind one edge to make a codex. The codices were easier to handle, and they gradually replaced the scrolls.

Materials: white or tan construction paper, tea, clothespins, clothesline or string, large needle, heavy thread

Guide the children in the following:
- Tear a sheet of construction paper into four equal parts.
- Dip the torn sheets into tea to make it look aged.
- Hang the sheets to dry.
- Place dry sheets on top of each other.
- Sew one edge using a needle and heavy thread to make a book (codex).

Kids Move

KEEP IT UP
(GROUP)
Materials: blown-up balloon

Divide the children into small groups of three or four, give each group a balloon, then **guide them in the following:**
- Name the books of the New Testament in order and tap the balloon in the air.
- Don't let the balloon touch the ground.

DROPPED A LETTER
(GROUP)
Many of the New Testament books are letters to the early churches.

Materials: plain fabric square to use as handkerchief, fine fabric marker

Ahead of time, use a fabric marker to write the names of the New Testament letters (Romans to Jude) onto one piece of fabric. Use this as the letter that is dropped during the game. The game is based on "I wrote a letter" or "Drop the handkerchief."
- One person is IT. The rest sit in a circle.
- IT walks around the outside of the circle, holding the handkerchief.
- The group sings or chants this song: "Paul wrote some letters to the church, but on the way he dropped it. One of you picked it up and put it in your pocket."
- At this point, IT drops the handkerchief behind someone.
- This person runs around the circle in the opposite direction, trying to reach his or her spot before IT.
- The last person back to the open spot is IT for the following round.

REORDER THE BOOKS
(GROUP OR PARTNERS)
Materials: New Testament index cards, clothesline string, clothespins

Ahead of time, write all the names of the New Testament books onto index cards, one book per card.
Then guide the children in the following:
- Mix up the cards, then put them back in order.
- A clothesline can be strung across the room, and children can clip the cards in order onto the line.

TIP
Keep the New Testament index cards for subsequent sessions. They will be used to play a variety of games.

GOOD NEWS TAG
(GROUP)
- One person is IT and is called the Good News Spreader. When IT tags someone else, this person joins hands with IT, and they work together to tag others. This game continues until everyone has "caught" the good news and has joined hands with IT.

Closing
For closing ideas, see page 7.

LETTER POUCH TEMPLATE

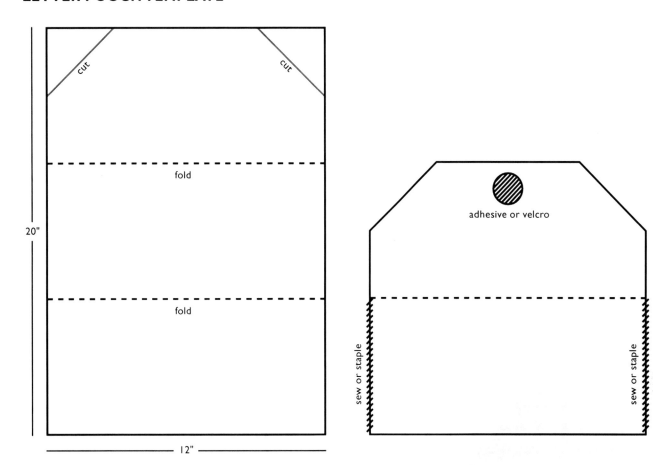

20"

cut

cut

fold

fold

12"

adhesive or velcro

sew or staple

sew or staple

Session 3
Messages in the Bible

(3)

The Bible is a very special book containing messages about God and God's people. These stories give us a picture of who God is. God is made known to the world through Jesus Christ, God's son.

BIBLE TEXT
Genesis, Judges, Matthew, Acts

FAITH CHALLENGE
We explore the story of God's people in the Bible.

ADVANCE PREPARATION
- Read through the entire session and decide what you will do.
- Set up the room/space for the various activities.
- Gather supplies for the craft or games you choose.
- Prepare a snack (see p. 14).

Kids Cluster

1. **Plan an activity for the early arrivals.** Check page 6 for ideas.
2. **Welcome the children, and gather for a time of singing** (p. 8). Be sure to include action songs, familiar songs, favorite songs, and new songs.

Kids Dig the Bible

1. **Begin with the theme song or a simple prayer.**
2. **Introduce the theme of the day:** We explore different types of writing in the Bible.
3. **For thousands of years,** many people would have only heard the scriptures read aloud. They would not have been able to read it. In Jesus' time, the Old Testament scriptures were read aloud from scrolls. The early churches read aloud the Old Testament scriptures and letters from other churches. Stories were told aloud and passed on from generation to generation.
4. **The Bible contains many, many stories,** but the overall story is about God and God's people. Today's story is a summary of several main themes in the biblical story. For each theme, a group will act out or make a frozen tableau scene to show the ideas that are read aloud. These messages or themes from the Bible start in the Old Testament (A, B, C, D) and end in the New Testament (E, F).

Divide your group into five smaller groups for these scenes. If your group is small, have the entire group act out each scene. Consider supplying the groups with props to use in their scenes.

A. **God creates:** God creates a beautiful world with every living creature imaginable, including people. God is happy with what God creates. God says it is very good!
B. **God calls a people:** God calls Abraham and Sarah to move to an unknown place. God promises to be with them and bless them with children and land. God calls Moses to lead the Israelite people to the Promised Land. God makes a covenant, or promise, with the people. God promises to be with them and bless them if they keep God's commands.
C. **God gives the people the law:** God calls Moses to lead the Israelite people to the Promised Land. God makes a covenant or promise with the people. God promises to be with them and bless them if they keep God's commands. God gives the people rules to live by.
D. **God judges and redeems a nation:** God's people do not always walk with God. Sometimes they follow their own ways. They turn away from God and worship idols. They disobey God's commands. God judges them. God also saves them from their enemies.
E. **God sends Jesus:** Jesus comes into the world to show a new way to understand God's promise, the same promise given to Abraham and Sarah. The Old Testament scriptures are very important to Jesus. Jesus teaches the Old Testament law in a different way. Many people follow Jesus as he teaches people and invites them to live in God's way.
F. **God's Spirit encourages a church:** After Jesus leaves, God sends God's Spirit to be with God's people. God invites the early Christian church to continue the work that Jesus began, showing others the way to God.

5. **Recite the books of the Bible in order, using songs** (p. 10). Help children distinguish between books of the Bible found in the Old and New Testaments.

   Learn today's memory verse from Psalm 119:1: "Happy are those whose way is blameless, who walk in the law of the LORD." Use the ideas from page 12 for creative Bible memorization.

6. **The messages in the Bible have the power to change lives** and change communities. In some parts of the world and at different times in history, the Bible has been banned. Some people were not allowed to own or read a Bible. But the good news keeps on spreading! People read the Bible together in secret, sharing stories, memorizing Scripture, and learning God's word. If time permits, read "The Secret Church Grows" (p. 44) as well as the Bible poem (p. 44) about some of the main stories in the Bible.

Kids Create

PRINTING BLOCKS
(INDIVIDUAL)

Johann Gutenberg invented the first printing press. The first book he printed, in 1456, was a complete Bible. Since then, it has been possible for more people to own their own Bibles, and more and more people have learned to read. This printing block craft will show children the method behind the printing press.

Materials: small blocks of wood, string, white glue, paper, ink pad

Guide the children in the following:
- Write your name in large letters on a piece of paper, tracing heavily over the letters.
- Turn the paper over, and trace the name backward onto a block of wood.
- Glue string along the traced lines on the block of wood. Let dry.
- Press the block onto an ink pad.
- Stamp names onto pieces of paper.

Optional: Use alphabet letter stamps and an ink pad to spell out today's memory verse. Decorate around the border.

GOD'S WORD IS LIKE . . .
(INDIVIDUAL)

Children will create a symbol for God's word.

Materials: modeling clay or play dough

Guide the children in the following:
- Use modeling clay or play dough to make a symbol of God's word.
- Symbols can include a lamp or light, bread, seed, mirror, or other items.

BIBLE MESSAGES
(INDIVIDUAL)

Materials: construction paper, markers, colored pencils, pencils

Guide the children in illustrating the five story themes from the Bible:
- Divide a piece of construction paper into five sections, and print the following themes across the page: God creates, God calls a people, God judges and redeems a nation, God sends Jesus, God's Spirit encourages a church.
- Illustrate each of the themes.

DECODE THE MESSAGES
(INDIVIDUAL)

Material: photocopies of decoding sheet (p. 45)

Guide the children in the following:
- Unscramble biblical words on each line.
- Put the numbered letters into the boxes at the bottom of the page.
- Unscrambled word solutions: love, joy, peace, kindness, patience, obey, follow, listen, do, give, pray, hear. Numbered boxes solution: Love the Lord your God.

Kids Move

GOD'S WORD SPREADS
(GROUP)

This game is similar to "Octopus." Make a long line at each end of the playing area with masking tape or rope.

- One child is the caller. The caller stands in the middle of the playing area.
- The other players stand at one end, facing the caller.
- When the caller yells, "God's word is spreading!" all players must run to the other side of the playing area.
- The caller attempts to tag as many of the players as possible. Anyone who is tagged joins the caller in the middle and helps to tag more players.
- Play until everyone has been tagged.

SECRET CHURCH SARDINES
(GROUP)

At different times in history, people have had to worship and read the Bible in secret.

Materials: several Bibles

Play a game like "Sardines," pretending to look for the secret church hiding spot.

- One child (IT) carries several small Bibles and hides, while the others close their eyes and count to twenty.
- Everyone searches for IT. When a player finds IT, she or he has found the secret church. She or he joins IT.
- They wait quietly for the others to join, paging through the Bibles that IT has brought along.

Closing

For closing ideas, see page 7.

OLD OR NEW?
(SMALL GROUP)

Materials: set of index cards with books of the Bible (Old and New Testament) written on them, one book per card

Guide the children in the following:
- Turn all of the cards upside down.
- Take turns turning over a card.
- When it is turned over, the child says the name printed on the card, then tells whether it is found in the Old or New Testament.
- If the child is correct, he or she keeps the card. If the child is incorrect, the card is turned face down on the playing area.

TIP

Keep these Bible index cards for games in other sessions.

PRISONER'S BASE
(GROUP)

Many people have been imprisoned for their beliefs or for reading the Bible.

Materials: two large, soft balls

- Divide the children into two teams of at least eight players each.
- Make boundary lines for each team about 45 ft. / 13 m apart and about 25 ft. / 7 m long. Divide the space with a line, with one team on either side.
- Each team starts with at least one large (preferably soft) ball. When a signal is given, players may throw the ball at the opposing team, trying to hit them below the waist.
- If a player is hit, he or she goes to the other team's "prison," which is behind their playing area.
- Play continues until one team is entirely in the other team's prison.

43

"THE SECRET CHURCH GROWS"
FROM *PLANT A SEED OF PEACE*
by Rebecca Seiling (Herald Press, 2007)

It was a dangerous time for the Mennonite church in Ethiopia. People were only allowed to follow the state religions; it was against the law to be a Mennonite. But many people wanted to join, because they liked what the Mennonites taught. The Mennonite church was called "Meserete Kristos," which means "Christ the Foundation." And it had 5,000 members. Their lives were in danger, because they were disobeying the law.

And the church kept growing.

Life got even harder for the Mennonite church. The government took the church's money and land, and stopped its programs. They wanted to destroy the Mennonite church, and any other church that didn't follow their instructions.

And the church kept growing.

It was dangerous to be caught with a Bible. If someone was found carrying a Bible, the government burned the Bible and put the person in prison. So people hid their Bibles and shared them. They tore sections out of the Bible, read them and memorized the words, then passed them on to a friend. When they gathered together, the people discussed what they had read and learned.

And the church kept growing.

The government took away the church's buildings, so people worshipped secretly in each other's homes. They read Scripture quietly and prayed. There was no loud singing—that was too dangerous.

And the church kept growing.

Someone always stood guard outside the home where people were meeting, watching for soldiers. One day, a soldier came up to the house and asked, "What's going on inside there?" The guard answered, "It's just a man talking to his sons." This was true—a man was talking to his sons. But the guard didn't tell the soldier what the man was talking about!

And the church kept growing.

The more the government persecuted the church, the more it grew. It was illegal to share your faith with others, but this didn't stop the Mennonites. They kept on inviting neighbors and coworkers to their meetings. They wanted to share the good news of Jesus, even though it was dangerous.

And the church kept growing.

After 10 years, a new government took power in Ethiopia. These leaders allowed the Mennonites to come out from hiding and worship the way they wanted. When they counted how many people were in the Mennonite church, they found there were more than 50,000 members! And thousands more were waiting to be baptized. By 1995, the Meserete Kristos church had more than 80,000 members. And now they could build church buildings and worship freely.
And the church kept growing.

"MESSAGES IN THE BIBLE"
(author unknown)

God made
Adam bit
Noah arked
Abraham split
Joseph ruled
Jacob fooled
Bush talked
Moses balked
Pharaoh plagued
People walked
Sea divided
Tablets guided
Promise landed
Prophets warned
Jesus born
God walked
Love talked
Anger crucified
Hope died
Love rose
Spirit flamed
Word spread
God remained.

DECODING SHEET

☺	☹	☼	☾	★	flower	tree	bird	bug
A	D	E	F	G	H	I	L	M

✶(person)	△	▽	○	■	□	●	▲	▼
N	O	P	R	S	T	U	W	Y

▼ △ ● ○   ▲ △ ○ ☺
__ __ __ __   __ __ __ __

tree ■ ☺ bird ☺ bug ▽
__ __ __ __ __ __ __

□ △ bug ▼ ☾ ☼ ☼ □
__ __ __ __ __ __ __ __

☺ (person) ☹ ☺ bird tree ★ flower □
__ __ __ __ __ __ __ __ __

□ △ bug ▼ ▽ ☺ □ flower
__ __ __ __ __ __ __ __

Session 4
A library in one book

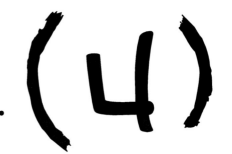

The Greek word biblios means "books," and it is also the origin of our English word Bible. Today we see the Bible as one book. However, for many years, the Bible was a collection of scrolls, letters, and codices (sheets of papyrus sewn together). The Bible that we now hold in our hands and read is a library of sixty-six in one book, a collection of writings from many places and time periods, originally written in Hebrew, Greek, and Aramaic. Imagine the countless hours of work that went into writing and then copying these writings and then translating them into many languages!

BIBLE TEXT
Psalm 119:9

FAITH CHALLENGE
We discover different types of writing in the Bible.

ADVANCE PREPARATION
- Read through the entire session and decide what you will do.
- Set up the room/space for the various activities.
- Make signs for the various sections of the Old Testament with simple pictures to illustrate (see below).
- On poster board, list the books of the Old Testament, divided into writing categories (see below).
- Gather supplies for the craft or games you choose.
- Prepare a snack (p. 14).

Kids Cluster

1. **Plan an activity for the early arrivals.** Check page 6 for ideas.
2. **Welcome the children, and gather for a time of singing** (p. 8). Be sure to include action songs, familiar songs, favorite songs, and new songs.
3. **Begin with the theme song or an opening prayer.**
4. **Introduce today's theme:** We discover different types of writing in the Bible.

Kids Dig the Bible

1. **The Bible is a collection of different types of writing.** For this activity, children will learn the various types of writing in the Old Testament. Put signs in four different areas of the room with simple pictures as follows:
   1. Books of the Law (lamp)
   2. Books of Poetry (praying hands)
   3. Books of Prophets (an open mouth with two hands cupped around it)
   4. Books of History (a storybook)

Post a list of the books of the Old Testament divided into the following categories: Books of the Law (Genesis through Deuteronomy), Books of History (Joshua through Esther), Books of Poetry (Job through Song of Solomon), Books of the Prophets (Isaiah through Malachi).

Ahead of time, post the four pictures around the room. Ask the children if they noticed the different signs in the room. Tell them that each sign represents a group of books in the Old Testament; each picture helps us to remember something about that group. As you talk about each group of books, move to that sign in the room.

Books of the Law: The Books of the Law are like a lamp lighting our way. The stories from Genesis and Exodus teach us God's ways. The Books of the Law set up rules for us to live by for a safe life that pleases God and lives in harmony with others. The Books of the Law include instructions and teaching through stories.

Books of Poetry: Praying hands represent prayers. Psalms is a book of prayers, songs, and poems. Many of the psalms are about joyfulness and thankfulness to God. Some psalms are also sad and mournful, and ask God questions about why things have happened. Other books in this section contain poetry or wise teachings and proverbs.

Books of the Prophets: The hands and mouth represent somebody calling out. The prophets called out to people to change their ways to follow in God's ways. The Books of the Prophets warned people that they needed to make changes in their lives, or there would be consequences.

Books of History: The storybook represents the Books of History. These books are stories about how the Israelite people lived in the land promised to Abraham. This was a time of kings, like King David and King Solomon, and judges, like Deborah. Stories include bravery, battles, and people striving to follow God.

Read aloud the following sentences. The children will listen to a sentence, then move to the picture in the room that represents that type of biblical writing.

Explain that these stories are in the section called the Books of the Law because God's ways and teachings were taught through rules as well as stories.

Tip
. . . .
When children move to the wrong section, make this a teachable moment. Children may naturally want to place some of the stories from Genesis and Exodus in the Books of History section.

1. God created the world. (Genesis, law)
2. Make a joyful noise to the Lord! Shout to the Lord with gladness! (Psalms, poetry)
3. Moses helped God bring the Israelites out of slavery in Egypt. (Exodus, law)
4. The words of the mouth are deep waters; the fountain of wisdom is a gushing stream. (Proverbs, poetry)
5. The people of Israel marched around the city of Jericho, and it was destroyed. (Joshua, history)
6. You shall not steal. (Leviticus, law)
7. Seek the Lord while he may be found, call upon him while he is near. (Isaiah, prophets)
8. Naomi and her daughter-in-law, Ruth, returned to the country of Moab. (Ruth, history)
9. The wise have eyes in their head, but fools walk in darkness. (Ecclesiastes, poetry)
10. Return, O Israel, to the Lord your God, for you have stumbled because of your iniquity. (Hosea, prophets)

2. **Sing "Genesis"** (p. 10). Divide the group into four according to the categories of writing in the Old Testament. Have the group stand when a book from their category is sung (for example, the Books of Prophets group stands when "Isaiah" is sung).

3. **Talk about the Bible.** Show a patchwork quilt to the group. Talk about how the Bible is like a patchwork quilt. There can be different patches from different times in history. Examine the patterns on the fabric of the quilt. How are these like the types of writing in the Bible? Some writing is more "flowery," some is plain. Some patches hold stories. Perhaps one fabric is from someone's favorite dress before it was made into a quilt piece, or another fabric is from a pillow. All the patches are put together to make a useful product in the form of a quilt.

   How is this like the Bible? Important and favorite stories, letters, and poems were put together over time to produce the Bible. Each piece is important and tells its own story. But working together, they tell the larger story of God walking with a people.

   The New Testament has different types of writing as well. The first four books are referred to as the Gospels. The book of Acts is considered a book of history that tells the story of the early churches. The following books (Romans through Jude) were written as letters to the first churches. The last book, Revelation, is a book of revelation.

4. **Practice reciting the books of the Old and New Testaments in order.**

   Recite together today's Bible memory verse from Psalm 119:9: "How can young people keep their way pure? By guarding it according to your word."

Tip
The early followers of Jesus were some of the first people to write on both sides of a paper and put material between two covers.

Kids Create

BIBLE BROWNIES
(GROUP)

Children will make a jar mix of brownies to give away. Before making this mix, children will practice looking up books in the Bible to find out which ingredients to use. Bake one batch of brownies and share them together during this time.

Materials: brownie ingredients as listed, quart jars, small recipe cards with these instructions: "Add 2/3 cup / 150 ml cooking oil, 4 eggs, and 2 tsp. / 10 ml vanilla to brownie mix. Mix well. Spread in 9 x 13 in. pan. Bake at 350 degrees F / 180 degrees C for 20 minutes. Enjoy!"

1 1/3 cup / 325 ml 1 Samuel 28:24 (flour)
2 cup / 500 ml Jeremiah 6:20 ("sweet cane," or sugar)
3/4 cup / 175 ml 1 Kings 10:1-2 ("spices," or cocoa)
1 tsp. / 5 ml Matthew 16:6 ("yeast," or baking powder)
1/2 tsp. / 2 ml Ezekiel 43:24 (salt)
1/2 cup / 125 ml Genesis 43:11 (nuts, such as walnuts)
2/3 cup / 150 ml 2 Kings 4:2 (oil)
4 Jeremiah 17:11a (eggs)
2 tsp. / 10 ml 2 Kings 20:13 ("spices," or vanilla)

- List the measurements and Scripture references on a poster with a blank line for each ingredient.
- Partner children so that readers can help non-readers. Have them take turns looking up references, then writing ingredient in the blank on poster.
- When the children have discovered all the ingredients, give each one a jar.

Guide the children in the following:
- Layer the first six brownie ingredients in a jar as follows: flour, sugar, cocoa, baking powder, salt, and walnuts.
- Add a recipe card with instructions.
- Screw on a lid.

FILL IN THE BOOKS
(INDIVIDUAL)

Materials: photocopies of page 11, pencils, Bibles

Guide the children in the following:
- Look in Bibles to fill in the missing books of the Bible in order.
- Color code the list according to the types of literature in the Bible: law, history, poetry and wisdom, prophets, gospels, acts, letters, prophecy.

BOOKS OF THE BIBLE BOOKMARK
(INDIVIDUAL)

Materials: eight different colors of card stock, photocopies of page 11, glue sticks, markers, hole punch, yarn, photocopies of page 54

Guide the children in the following:
- Cut apart photocopies of the writing categories of the Bible: Books of the Law (Genesis through Deuteronomy), Books of History (Joshua through Esther), Books of Poetry (Job through Song of Solomon), Books of the Prophets (Isaiah through Malachi), Gospels (Matthew through John), Church beginnings (Acts), Letters (Romans through Jude), Revelation (Revelation).
- Cut eight different colors of card stock into a bookmark strip for the each categories of literature in the Bible.
- Print a category title on each bookmark.
- Glue photocopied list of books onto each bookmark, and decorate with drawings.
- Punch holes in the tops of the eight bookmarks.
- Tie yarn through the holes.

MAKING PAPYRUS
(INDIVIDUAL)

Scrolls were written on either papyrus or parchment. Papyrus was a reed plant that grew on riverbanks. The reeds were sliced into thin strips. Several strips were laid side by side, then another layer was placed on top horizontally. The layers were pounded together to make papyrus paper. This craft gives children the chance to experience part of this process.

Materials: plates, mixture of glue thinned with water, tissue, waxed paper, paper towels
Cover the children's work surface with waxed paper, and place the water-and-glue mixture on plates.

Guide the children in the following:
- Tear a tissue into wide strips, keeping together the double thickness.
- Dip the strips of tissue one by one into the water-and-glue mixture.
- Lay four or five strips next to each other, overlapping slightly.
- Lay other strips horizontally on top of them.
- Press the "papyrus" gently with a paper towel to remove moisture.
- Let dry overnight.

Kids Move

BOOKS OF THE BIBLE MEMORY GAME
(SMALL GROUP)
Ahead of time, create two sets of Bible book cards by writing one name of a book of the Bible on two index cards. Do this with all the books.
- Turn cards upside down.
- Players take turns flipping over two cards.
- If a book match is found, that player keeps those cards.

BIBLE BOOKS UPSET
(GROUP)
This game is played like "Fruit basket upset."

Set chairs or mats in a circle, enough for everyone in the group except one.
- One person (IT) stands in the middle of the circle, and the others sit on a chair or mat.
- Each circle member is given a name of a book of the Bible from a specific writing group (for example, Genesis, Exodus, Leviticus, Numbers). There will be several children with each book name.
- IT calls out one of these books ("Numbers!"), and all the people with that name stand up, find another spot, and sit down.
- The person who remains without a seat is IT. When IT calls out the category of writing ("Law!"), everyone stands and changes seats.

WHAT CATEGORY
(GROUP)
- Use one set of Bible book cards (see "Books of the Bible Memory Game" above). Mix the cards, and give each child several until all of the cards are handed out.
- Set out Bible category cards on the floor: law, history, psalms and wisdom, prophets, gospels, acts, letters, revelation. Go around the circle, and have each child put one of his or her cards into the right category.
- Continue until all cards are categorized.

STORY BLANKET
Materials: story Bible, large blanket

- Children choose a Bible story and use the story blanket as their only prop to act it out. The blanket can be a river, a robe, a tent, a burning bush, or other object.
- Give children a story Bible, and one child can act as the narrator. Other children can act out the character parts as they are read.

Closing
For closing ideas, see page 7.

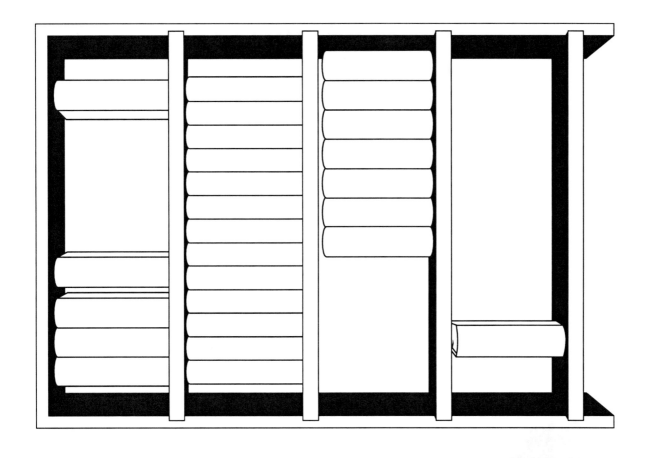

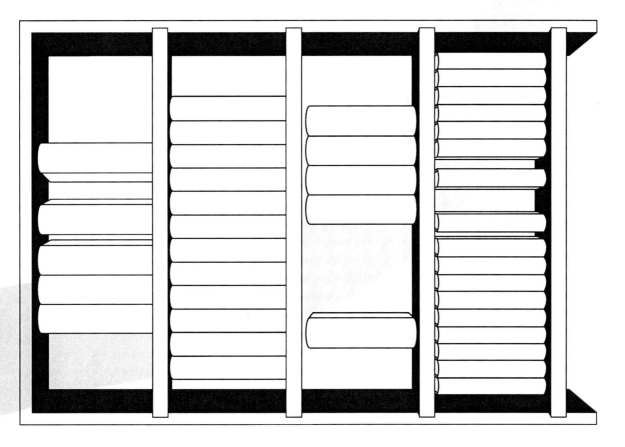

Old Testament

BOOKS OF THE LAW

Genesis
Exodus
Leviticus
Numbers
Deuteronomy

BOOKS OF HISTORY

Joshua
Judges
Ruth
1 Samuel
2 Samuel
1 Kings
2 Kings
1 Chronicles
2 Chronicles
Ezra
Nehemiah
Esther

BOOKS OF POETRY

Job
Psalms
Proverbs
Ecclesiastes
Song of Solomon

BOOKS OF THE PROPHETS

Isaiah
Jeremiah
Lamentations
Ezekiel
Daniel
Hosea
Joel
Amos
Obadiah
Jonah
Micah
Nahum
Habakkuk
Zephaniah
Haggai
Zechariah
Malachi

New Testament

GOSPELS

Matthew
Mark
Luke
John

CHURCH BEGINNINGS

Acts of the Apostles

LETTERS

Romans
1 Corinthians
2 Corinthians
Galatians
Ephesians
Philippians
Colossians
1 Thessalonians
2 Thessalonians
1 Timothy
2 Timothy
Titus
Philemon
Hebrews
James
1 Peter
2 Peter
1 John
2 John
3 John
Jude

REVELATION

Revelation

Session 5
God's promises

(5)

There are many promises in the Bible—covenants that God makes with individuals and with the people of Israel, promises in the Psalms and Prophets, and promises in the New Testament writings. We can extend God's promises in the Bible to children as they learn what it means to live as children of God.

BIBLE TEXT
Genesis 6:18; 9:11; 12:2-7; Jeremiah 29:11; 31:31-34

FAITH CHALLENGE
We discover God's promises to us in the Bible.

ADVANCE PREPARATION
- Read through the entire session and decide what you will do.
- Set up the room/space for the various activities.
- Gather storytelling props: drawing of a rainbow, star stickers on black paper, a red paper heart with the words "I will always be with you" written on it.
- Gather supplies for the craft or games you choose.
- Prepare a snack (p. 14).

Kids Cluster

1. **Plan an activity for the early arrivals.** Check page 6 for ideas.
2. **Welcome the children, and gather for a time of singing** (p. 8). Be sure to include action songs, familiar songs, favorite songs, and new songs.
3. **Begin with the theme song or an opening prayer.**
4. **Introduce today's theme:** We discover God's promises to us in the Bible.

Kids Dig the Bible

1. **There are many promises in the Bible.** Discuss promises the children have made. Have they made a promise to someone? Have they ever broken a promise? Today's story will summarize several promises found in the Old Testament to Noah, Abraham and Sarah, and the Israelite people.

2. **Turn to Genesis and Jeremiah** in your Bible to show children where the stories are found. Hold up the following props as you tell the story: drawing of a rainbow (Noah story), star stickers on a black piece of construction paper (Abraham and Sarah story), and a red construction paper heart with the words "I will always be with you" written on it (Israelite people story). You could have children hold up each prop when it is needed.

   Ask the children to practice the following with you, explaining that they will be saying it several times during the storytelling: "God's book of promises is God's word. God made many promises. Have you heard?" Give them a signal that you will use for them to recite these lines in the story.

   Children: God's book of promises is God's word.
   God made many promises. Have you heard?

   God promised to save Noah from the great big flood. Noah and his family were kept safe in the ark because they obeyed God. At the end of the flood, God made another promise to Noah: that God would never again send a flood that would destroy the whole earth. God remembered this promise by placing a rainbow in the sky.

   Children: God's book of promises is God's word.
   God made many promises. Have you heard?

   God promised to bless Abraham and Sarah. God promised that they would become a great nation, and that they would be a blessing to many others. God also promised Abraham land. God promised that Abraham and Sarah would have a baby, even in their old age. In fact, God promised that they would have so many descendants, they would be as numerous as the stars in the sky.

   Children: God's book of promises is God's word.
   God made many promises. Have you heard?

   God made a new promise with the Israelite people. God promised, "I will be with you always. I will give you hope and a future." God promised to put God's law within them and to write it on their hearts. God said, "I will be your God, and you will be my people."

   Children: God's book of promises is God's word.
   God made many promises. Have you heard?

3. **Discuss God's promises with the children:** We heard stories of God's promises to others in the Bible. Imagine how Noah or Abraham or Sarah felt when God made a promise to them. Imagine how they felt when they realized that God had kept that promise. What promises does God make with us today?

4. **Recite the books of the Bible in order, using the songs** (p. 10) to help. Learn today's memory verse from Psalm 12:6a: "The promises of the LORD are promises that are pure." Use the ideas on page 12 to memorize Scripture.

5. **As they work or eat a snack,** share the story "Water in a Coal Basket" (p. 60) with the group.

> **Tip**
> ·················
> Consider using a felt board with felt shapes of a rainbow, stars, and a heart to tell this story. Visual aids will help children remember these specific promises in the Bible.

Kids Create

PROMISE CANS
(INDIVIDUAL)
Children will decorate cans and fill them with verses that show them God's promises in the Bible.

Materials: photocopies of page 60, cans with plastic lids (chip or coffee cans), paper, scissors, glue, markers, gem stickers, sequins, etc.

Guide the children in the following:
- Cut page 60 into strips, and curl or fold them so that the verses can be put into the can
- Decorate a can using crafts supplies. Include the words "Promises in the Bible."

RAINBOW MOBILE
(INDIVIDUAL)
Children will make a rainbow reminder of God's promise to never again flood the whole earth.

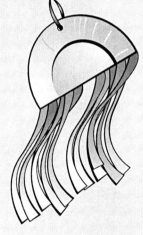

Materials: paper plates, paper streamers in rainbow colors (red, orange, yellow, green, blue, purple), scissors, white glue, ribbon for hanging

Guide the children in the following:
- Cut paper plates in half.
- Cut a 40-in. / 100-cm piece of streamer in each color.
- Glue the red strip along the top edge of the paper plate. Center the streamer so that there are equal parts hanging off the bottom of the plate.
- Repeat with each color in this order: red, orange, yellow, green, blue, purple.
- Make a hole in the top, and thread a piece of ribbon through.
- Knot the ribbon to hang the mobile.

ILLUMINATE PSALM 23
(INDIVIDUAL)
God is like a shepherd, staying with us even during hard, dark times. During the Middle Ages, monks decorated or "illuminated" manuscripts of the Bible. Many monks devoted their lives to studying the Scriptures and copying the text. They made drawings of objects or scenes that highlighted important events or features of the text. Children will illuminate the passage of Psalm 23.

Materials: photocopies of Psalm 23 (p. 59) typed in a fancy font with wide margins for children to draw, markers, colored pencils

Guide the children in the following:
- Illuminate, or decorate, the page by drawing objects and scenes from the text.

STAR PROMISE BRACELET
(INDIVIDUAL)
Children will be reminded of God's promise to Abraham and Sarah to give them as many descendants as the stars in the sky.

Materials: 3/8-in. / 1-cm vinyl tubing, ¼-in. / 1/2-cm vinyl tubing, funnel, scissors, star sprinkles (used for cake decorating)
Ahead of time, for each bracelet cut 8 in. / 20 cm of 3/8-in. / 1-cm vinyl tubing and 1 in. / 2.5 cm of ¼-in. / 1/2-cm tubing.

Guide pairs of children in the following:
- Place a finger over one end of the large piece of tubing, and put the funnel in the other end.
- Pour star sprinkles through the funnel into the tubing.
- To seal the bracelet, bend the large tubing around so that you can attach both ends to the small piece of tubing.

Optional: Children put rainbow sprinkles into the tubing to remind them of God's rainbow promise to Noah.

Kids Move

PASS THE BIBLE
(GROUP)

Use this game, similar to "Pass the Potato," to review books of the Bible.

Materials: Bible, music

- Sit or stand in a circle.
- Pass a Bible around the circle while music plays.
- When the music stops, the one with the Bible names a book of the Bible.
- Children are "out" when they name a book not found in the section of the Bible that is chosen.
- Make the game more challenging by asking for only Old or New Testament books.

LIGHTHOUSE
(GROUP)

Seeing a lighthouse gives sailors courage in a storm. It is a signal that they are safe and near land. This game can remind children of the promise that God is with us and can give us courage during hard times.

Materials: Bible, blindfolds

- One child is the Lighthouse. The Lighthouse stands on one side of the room.
- The other players are in two groups: rocks and ships. Rocks spread out around the room, sitting on the floor.
- Ships wear blindfolds and start walking at one side of the room, opposite the Lighthouse. The goal is for the ships to walk to the Lighthouse without touching the rocks.
- The Lighthouse makes a beeping noise for the ships to follow, while the rocks make a noise like water on rocks. If a ship touches a rock, the ship sinks and sits by the rock.
- When all ships have sunk or reached the Lighthouse, switch roles.

PROMISEBALL
(GROUP)

Sometimes it might be hard to remember God's promises, or to see them in your life. This game surprises players as the balloon comes over the net. God's promises can surprise us too.

Materials: bed sheet, two chairs, masking tape, inflated balloon

- Spread a bed sheet between two chairs to create a net. Tape it securely so that it hangs vertically.
- Divide the group into two teams. Players sit on the floor, facing the net.
- One team starts with the balloon. They hit the balloon over the net.
- The receiving team must hit it twice among teammates before hitting it back over the net.
- If a team drops the balloon on the ground, the opposing team gets one point.

GOD LOVES ...
(GROUP)

Children can remember the promise of God's steadfast love through this game.

Materials: blindfold

- One person is IT and wears a blindfold.
- The other players move around the playing area, trying not to get caught by IT.
- IT calls out "God loves . . ." and the other players respond with "me!"
- IT follows the voices and tries to tag another player.
- The tagged player becomes IT for the next round.

Optional: To make this game easier for younger children, have the players freeze as IT walks around.

Closing
For closing ideas, see page 7.

58

Psalm 23
The Divine Shepherd

A Psalm of David

The Lord is my shepherd, I shall not want.
   He makes me lie down in green pastures;
he leads me beside still waters;
   he restores my soul.
he leads me in right paths
   for his name's sake.

Even though I walk through the darkest valley,
   I fear no evil;
for you are with me.
   your rod and your staff—
   they comfort me.

You prepare a table before me
   in the presence of my enemies;
you anoint my head with oil;
   my cup overflows.
Surely goodness and mercy shall follow me
   all the days of my life,
and I shall dwell in the house of the Lord
   my whole life long.

PROMISES
(FOR PROMISE CANS)

"For surely I know the plans I have for you, says the LORD, plans for your welfare and not for harm, to give you a future with hope. Then when you call upon me and come and pray to me, I will hear you. When you search for me, you will find me; if you seek me with all your heart." **Jeremiah 29:11-13**

"The LORD will guide you continually, and satisfy your needs in parched places, and make your bones strong; and you shall be like a watered garden, like a spring of water, whose waters never fail." **Isaiah 58:11**

"Even though I walk through the darkest valley, I fear no evil; for you are with me; your rod and your staff—they comfort me." **Psalm 23:4**

"Peace I leave with you; my peace I give to you. I do not give to you as the world gives. Do not let your hearts be troubled, and do not let them be afraid." **John 14:27**

"For the LORD is good; his steadfast love endures forever, and his faithfulness to all generations." **Psalm 100:5**

"WATER IN A COAL BASKET"
Author unknown

Each morning, Grandpa was up early sitting at the kitchen table, reading from his old, worn-out Bible. His grandson, who wanted to be just like him, tried to imitate him in any way he could.

One day the grandson asked, "Papa, I try to read the Bible just like you, but I don't understand it, and what I do understand I forget as soon as I close the book. What good does reading the Bible do?" The grandfather quietly turned from putting coal in the stove and said, "Take this coal basket down to the river. Bring back a basket of water."

The boy did as he was told. But all the water leaked out before he could get back to the house. The grandfather laughed and said, "You will have to move a little faster next time," and sent him back to the river to try again.

This time the boy ran faster. Again, the basket was empty before he returned home. Out of breath, he told his grandfather, "It is impossible to carry water in a basket!" The boy went to get a bucket instead. The old man said, "I don't want a bucket of water. I want a basket of water. You can do this." He went out the door to watch the boy try again.

At this point, the boy knew it was impossible, but he wanted to show his grandfather that even if he ran as fast as he could, the water would leak out before he got very far. The boy scooped the water and ran hard, but when he reached his grandfather, the basket was empty.

Out of breath, he said, "See, Papa, it's useless!"

The old man said, "So you think it is useless? Look at the basket." The boy looked at the basket, and for the first time he realized that the basket looked different. Instead of a dirty old coal basket, it was clean. "Son, that's what happens when you read the Bible. You might not understand or remember everything. But when you read it, it will change you from the inside out."

Session 6
Life in Bible times

(6)

• •

What do you know about life in the ancient world more than two thousand years ago? In today's session, children will get a glimpse into life during Bible times. The Bible stories can come alive in new ways when we understand more about the people, places, foods, and terrain of that time.

BIBLE TEXT
Luke 10:30-35

FAITH CHALLENGE
We imagine life in Bible times.

ADVANCE PREPARATION
• Read through the entire session and decide what you will do.
• Set up the room/space for the various activities.
• Gather storytelling props: map of Bible lands in Jesus' time, six bathrobes, cloth bandage.
• Gather supplies for the craft or games you choose.
• Prepare a snack (p. 14).

Kids Cluster

1. **Plan an activity for the early arrivals.** Check page 6 for ideas.
2. **Welcome the children, and gather for a time of singing** (p. 8). Be sure to include action songs, familiar songs, favorite songs, and new songs.
3. **Begin with the theme song or an opening prayer.**
4. **Introduce today's theme:** We imagine life in Bible times.

Kids Dig the Bible

1. **Have the children close their eyes.** Ask them to imagine their neighborhood. What do the streets look like? What is alongside the streets? Are there sidewalks or curbs, or just the shoulder of the road? Are there trees or buildings or parks? How do people travel along the street? Do they walk or ride bike? Are they inside a car or bus? What do people wear? Where do they go if they are hungry? Are there nearby restaurants or fast-food places? Pause and let children create this familiar scene in their mind.

   Ask them to imagine a very different scene by thinking about how Bible times are different from our time. Describe the following: dusty roads; people walking or riding donkeys; people passing by wearing leather sandals and long brown robes, their heads covered by shawls or veils; people carrying worn, leather bags; people stopping by the side of the dirt road to eat some flatbread; and farmers in fields in the distance. Houses had only a few rooms with many people living under one roof—brothers, sisters, grandparents, nieces, nephews, aunts, uncles, and servants too. Animals lived on the main floor of the house, and people slept on the roof when it was too hot. Pause and allow children to create this scene.

   Discuss the differences between the two scenes.

2. **Show a map of the Bible lands,** found in a Bible atlas or in maps at the back of your Bible. Point out some of the key places that children might recognize from stories: Jerusalem, Jericho, Samaria, Bethlehem, Nazareth, Sea of Galilee, Red Sea, Nile River, and Canaan. Use the map to tell the Bible story, and point to places such as Jerusalem, Jericho, and Samaria (where the Samaritan man was from).

3. **Open your Bible to Luke 10.** Show the children how to find Luke in the New Testament. Tell the story based on Luke 10:30-35, having children act it out as you tell it. There are several parts: Samaritan man, group of robbers (two or three), a priest, a Levite, and a Samaritan man. Supply bathrobes for each character and a sling bandage or piece of fabric to bandage the wounded man.

   One day, a man asked Jesus, "Who is my neighbor?" This is the story Jesus told: "Once a man was going from Jerusalem to Jericho. A group of robbers pounced on the man, beat him, and went away. They left him to die alone on the road.

   By chance, a priest was walking down that same road. He saw the wounded man, but passed right on by.

   By chance, a Levite was walking down that same road. He saw the wounded man, but passed right on by.

   By chance, a Samaritan man was traveling on that same road. He saw the wounded man, and felt sorry for him. Right away he went to him to clean and bandage his wounds. The Samaritan man put the wounded man on his donkey and brought him to an inn to care for him.

Tip
. . . .
As an additional option, consider having a guest who has traveled to Israel/Palestine come to show slides or photos and talk to the group. This person could talk about how traveling there made the biblical stories come alive.

Tip
. . . .
Consider passing out acting parts to those who like to act to perform the skit "Jesus Tells the Story of the Good Samaritan" from *Fun Bible Skits!* by David M. Morrow (Scottdale, PA: Faith and Life Resources, 2005).

The next day the Samaritan man gave the innkeeper some money and said, "Take care of this man. When I come back, I will pay you back for whatever you spend on him."
"And so . . ." said Jesus, "Who is my neighbor?"

4. **Talk about the Bible**
    - Why did Jesus tell this story? Who was he talking to? What was he trying to teach?
    - Two men passed by the wounded man without helping him. Why do you think they did that?
    - There were rules around the duties that priests and Levites could perform. If they had touched the man, they could not perform their duties. In the time of Jesus, Samaritans were not trusted by people who lived in Jerusalem or Jericho. Yet this Samaritan man stopped to help someone who was not from his town. Why do you think he did that?
    - Imagine being the wounded man, watching people walk right by you without stopping to help. Have you or your parents ever stopped to help someone who needed help? How did it make you feel?
    - When Jesus was telling this story, he must have known that people would be surprised that a Samaritan stopped to help. Have you ever been surprised by someone doing something unexpectedly helpful?

5. **Work together to recite the books** of the Old and New Testaments in order. Use songs or games to memorize (see p. 10).

    Recite together today's Bible memory verse, Luke 10:27: "You shall love the Lord your God with all your heart, and with all your soul, and with all your strength, and with all your mind; and your neighbor as yourself."

6. **Read "An Unspoken Bible"** (p. 66) as the children work or eat a snack.

Tip
Use these questions/ ideas as conversation points during the craft time. It is not necessary to sit quietly and reflect on these points, but do include them during other activities.

Kids Create

BIBLE CHARACTER SCULPTURE
(INDIVIDUAL)

Children will use a variety of materials to make a Bible character. Look at pictures in books or online to note typical dress from that time period, and create similar clothing.

Materials: wire (multistrand telephone cable works well), cardboard or wooden blocks for base, small scraps of fabric, yarn, ribbon, hot glue

Guide the children in the following:
- Decide which Bible character to create. Wrap, bend, or shape wire to make a "skeleton" for the figure.
- Design and make a long robe like those in Jesus' day, and attach it to the wire skeleton.
- Attach the wire figure to the base, using hot glue gun (adult participation is required here).

EGG CARTON SCAVENGER HUNT
(GROUP)

Children will look through the Bible for clues and then find objects hidden around the room. If possible, have youth or adult helpers assigned to each group to find the references in the Bibles. Hide items for the scavenger hunt ahead of time. Photocopy the clues on page 67. Cut apart each set of clues, and glue one clue into each section of an egg carton. Prepare one carton for every two children in the group.

Materials: photocopies of clues, Bibles, prepared egg cartons, fish crackers, candy hearts, star stickers, salt packets, pebbles, sunflower seeds, small pieces of purple cloth, honey packets, grapes, "pearl" beads, dimes, pieces of leather

Guide the children in the following:
- Read the clues in the egg carton sections, and find the reference in a Bible.
- Search the room for the item that matches that answer.
- When the item is found, place it in the appropriate section of the egg carton.

MAKE A MAP
(GROUP)

Children will work together to create a relief map of the biblical lands were Jesus lived and taught.

Materials: salt dough (see recipe below), large piece of plywood with a map of Palestine during Jesus' time drawn on it (see p. 68), paper, straight pins or clear tape

Guide the children in the following:
- Use salt dough to create the mountains, hills, valleys, and seas of the area.
- Print names of significant places (Mediterranean Sea, Sea of Galilee, Jordan River, Dead Sea, Bethlehem, Jerusalem, Samaria, Nazareth, Capernaum, Cana, Jericho) onto small pieces of paper.
- Attach names to the map, using straight pins or clear tape.

Salt dough recipe
1 cup / 250 ml salt
2 cup / 500 ml flour
3/4 to 1 cup / 175 ml to 250 ml lukewarm water
Green and blue food coloring

Mix the salt and flour in a bowl, using a wooden spoon. Add the water until a large ball has formed. Knead at length on a lightly floured surface. Divide the dough into two parts: one for land and one for water. Add blue food coloring to the "water" and green food coloring to the "land."

FRIENDSHIP BRACELETS
(INDIVIDUAL)

Children will make a bracelet to give away to someone who has helped them, like the Samaritan man in Jesus' story.

Materials: colorful beads, lacing

Guide the children in the following:
- Braid and tie lacing to make a bracelet.
- Add beads by stringing the lacing through a bead and then knotting the lacing.

Kids Move

NOMADS AND SETTLERS
(GROUP)

This game shows the conflict between settled farmers and wandering shepherds during Bible times. This could relate to stories of the struggle for land and water in the Bible. Lot and Abraham had to figure out how to divide the land, and there were conflict over wells.

Materials: stones, sidewalk chalk
Ideally, this game is played outside on a paved area.

- Divide players into two groups: nomads and settlers.
- The settlers collect a pile of stones and put them inside the playing area. The settlers stand in a circle around the pile, holding hands. Mark a circle around settlers. This is the settlers' territory.
- The nomads draw another, much larger circle around the settlers' territory. This is the area where nomads are safe.
- The object of the game is for the nomads to seize the settlers' goods (stones) without being captured, and for the settlers to protect their goods. The nomads can charge the settlers' circle by pushing through or ducking under clasped hands. They may use only heads or shoulders to get in, not hands.
- When they collect some goods, they must be permitted to leave the circle, passing safely through the nomads' safe zone.
- When the nomads are outside the larger circle, the settlers may chase them.
- When the settlers touch the nomads with both hands on the nomad's backs, the settlers may take the goods back to the middle circle. A nomad who has been caught must remain outside of the settlers' circle.
- The game is over when the settlers have no more goods, or when all the nomads have been caught.

Tip

Children can enjoy a Bible-times snack (see p. 14 for ideas) as they play or create.

Closing

For closing ideas, see page 7.

SHEPHERD RELAY
(GROUP)

Many people worked as shepherds in Bible times, caring for and protecting a flock of sheep.

- Divide children into two teams. Have a bag with shepherd clothing (bathrobe, lengths of fabric, towel, sandals, walking stick) for each team.
- Mark two lines at either end of the playing space.
- Have teams line up behind one line. Set the clothing bags at the other line.
- At the signal, the first person on each team runs to the clothing bag, dresses up like a shepherd, says, "Where are you, sheep?" then puts the clothing back into the bag.
- The first person runs back to the team and tags the second person, and the relay continues.

BOAT TAG
(GROUP)

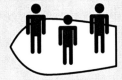
"IT"

Many people in Jesus' time traveled by boat or worked on boats catching fish.

Use masking tape to make boat shapes on the floor. For every five children in your group, make one boat shape.

- Everyone starts by standing in one boat, except for IT.
- IT calls out categories, such as "Kids wearing blue" or "Kids who like pizza."
- Those who fit the called category must run to a different boat. They are safe when they are in the boat.
- While they run, IT tries to tag them. Those who are tagged become IT too.
- When IT calls out, "Boats are sinking," children must all change boats.
- Start a new round when most of the players have been tagged.

"AN UNSPOKEN BIBLE"
Author unknown

His name is Bill. He has wild hair, wears a T-shirt with holes in it, jeans, and no shoes. Bill is a very smart college student who just decided to follow Jesus.

Across the street from the campus is a church. One day Bill decides to go there. He walks in with no shoes, jeans, his holey T-shirt, and wild hair. The service has already started, so Bill starts down the aisle, looking for a seat.

The church is completely packed, and he can't find a seat. People in the church are really looking a bit uncomfortable, but no one says anything. Bill gets closer and closer to the front pulpit. When he realizes there are no seats, he just squats down right on the carpet at the front. This had never happened in their church before.

People are wondering what will happen next. At this time, the minister realizes that from way at the back of the church, an elder is slowly making his way toward Bill. The elder is in his eighties, with silver-gray hair and a three-piece suit. He walks with a cane.

It takes a long time for the man to reach the student. The church is utterly silent except for the clicking of the man's cane. Even the minister has stopped speaking. All eyes are focused on this elderly man. The people watch as he drops his cane on the floor. With great difficulty he lowers himself and sits down next to Bill to worship with him.

People are touched with emotion. When the minister gains control, he says, "What I'm about to preach, you will never remember. What you have just seen, you will never forget. So be careful how you live. You may be the only Bible some people will ever read."

Before Peter and Andrew met Jesus they caught these. **Matthew 4:18-19**	God is _____. **1 John 1:5**	Abraham's descendants would be as numerous as _____. **Genesis 22:17**	You are the _____. **Matthew 5:13**
What helped the children of Israel remember what God had done for them? **Joshua 4:1-2; 21**	Jesus told a story about a farmer who went out to sow _____. **Mark 4:3**	Lydia was a dealer in _____. **Acts 16:14**	God's words are sweeter than _____. **Psalm 19:10**
This verse mentions a common fruit in the Bible. **Habakkuk 3:17**	The kingdom of heaven is like a merchant looking for _____. **Matthew 13:45-46**	Jesus told a parable about one of these that was lost. **Luke 15:8-10**	This was used to make water containers, scrolls, tents, and belts. **2 Kings 1:8**

EGG CARTON SCAVENGER HUNT CLUES

Before Peter and Andrew met Jesus they caught these. **Matthew 4:18-19**	God is _____. **1 John 1:5**	Abraham's descendants would be as numerous as _____. **Genesis 22:17**	You are the _____. **Matthew 5:13**
What helped the children of Israel remember what God had done for them? **Joshua 4:1-2; 21**	Jesus told a story about a farmer who went out to sow _____. **Mark 4:3**	Lydia was a dealer in _____. **Acts 16:14**	God's words are sweeter than _____. **Psalm 19:10**
This verse mentions a common fruit in the Bible. **Habakkuk 3:17**	The kingdom of heaven is like a merchant looking for _____. **Matthew 13:45-46**	Jesus told a parable about one of these that was lost. **Luke 15:8-10**	This was used to make water containers, scrolls, tents, and belts. **2 Kings 1:8**

Permission is granted to purchasers of *Kids Can Dig the Bible* to photocopy this page for use with this curriculum.

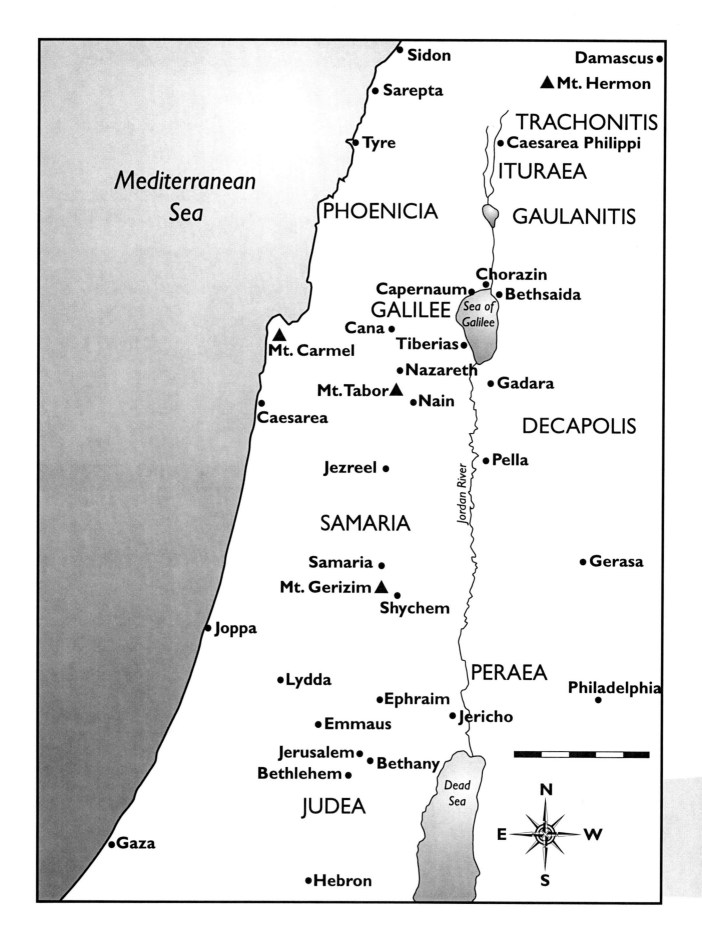

Session 7
Words in our hearts

(7)

Jesus asked his followers to listen. When we listen to and act on God's words in the Bible, we follow God's way for our lives. God desires that God's word be planted in our hearts, written like a message that we never forget. In this session, children can learn the importance of listening and remembering God's word.

BIBLE TEXT
Matthew 7:24-27

FAITH CHALLENGE
We listen to God's word and keep it in our hearts.

ADVANCE PREPARATION
- Read through the entire session and decide what you will do.
- Set up the room/space for the various activities.
- Gather storytelling props: sand, flat rocks (such as flagstone), pitcher of water, baking sheet, optional electric fan.
- Gather supplies for the craft or games you choose.
- Prepare a snack (p. 14).

Kids Cluster

1. **Plan an activity for the early arrivals.** Check page 6 for ideas.
2. **Welcome the children, and gather for a time of singing** (p. 8). Be sure to include action songs, familiar songs, favorite songs, and new songs.
3. **Begin with the theme song or an opening prayer.**
4. **Introduce today's theme:** We listen to God's word in the Bible and remember it.

Kids Dig the Bible

1. **Jesus often said, "Listen!" or "If you have ears, listen!"** Listening and acting on what was heard was important. In the language of the Bible, listening and acting were the same thing. If you heard something, but did not act on it, then you did not actually hear it. In today's story, Jesus talks about those who hear God's word and do something about it, and those who hear and do nothing.

   Play a listening game. In preparation, discuss good and bad listening skills. Bad listening skills can include looking away, yawning, talking, interrupting, or singing. Good listening skills can include eye contact, nodding, asking a question to clarify, and empathizing.

   - Pair children. One child will speak to the other for twenty seconds. While this child speaks, the other one uses poor listening skills.
   - Do this a second time, but this time the listener uses good listening skills.
   - Have the partners switch roles.

   Discuss what happened: Do you ever listen to someone, but you are not really listening? Sometimes our minds wander and we think about other things when we are supposed to be listening. Learning to listen well can be challenging, but it is something to strive for.

2. **Open your Bible to Matthew 7 to show where today's story is found.** Have the children practice lines to be used during the storytelling: "Open your ears. What do you hear? Listen to the word of God." Give them a signal that you will use to indicate it is time to say their lines.

   Set up storytelling props, including sand, flat rocks, and a pitcher of water. Use a baking sheet for the base as you tell the story. Pour water over the rocks or sand to represent the rain falling down. An electric fan could work well to represent wind. Tell the following story based on Matthew 7:24-27:

   Children: Open your ears. What do you hear? Listen to the word of God.

   Jesus said, "Everyone who hears my words and does something about them is like a wise man who built his house upon a rock. The rain came down, the winds blew, but the house on the rock did not fall, because it was built on the rock."

   Children: Open your ears. What do you hear? Listen to the word of God.

   Jesus said, "Everyone who hears my words and does nothing about them is like a foolish man who built his house on sand. The rain came down, the winds blew, and the house on the sand fell flat."

   Children: Open your ears. What do you hear? Listen to the word of God.

3. **Talk about the Bible**
   - How did the wise man know that he should build on the rock?
   - Why did the foolish man build on sand?
   - Our actions need to show that we are listening. When we listen, our behavior can change. Do you ever hear words that adults say, but do nothing about it? Why?
   - I wonder how we can listen for God's words in the Bible and do something about what we hear.

   Sing "The Wise Man Built His House Upon the Rock."

4. **Work on memorizing the books of the Old and New Testaments.**
   Recite together today's verse, Psalm 119:10: "With my whole heart I seek you; do not let me stray from your commandments."

5. **Read the poem "The Family Bible"** (p. 74). Do you have a Bible that is read at home? Are you like the Higgins or the Miggins in that poem?

   Read "The Bible in Their Hearts" (p. 74). Imagine your community memorizing the entire Bible together!

Tip
Use these questions/ideas as conversation points during the craft time. It is not necessary to sit quietly and reflect on these points, but do include them during other activities.

Kids Create

MEZUZAHS
(INDIVIDUAL)

A mezuzah is a tiny scroll that is kept in a little case. It usually contains words from Deuteronomy 6:4-5 (known as the shema). The Hebrew people attached mezuzahs to their door posts or door frames.

Materials: 1-in. / 2.5-cm clear plastic tubing cut into 7-in. / 18-cm pieces, permanent markers, glitter glue, paper, Bibles, double-sided tape

Guide the children in the following:
- Decorate the tubing with markers and glitter glue.
- Print Deuteronomy 6:4-5 on a small piece of paper.
- Curl the paper, and place it inside the tube.
- Add a piece of double-sided tape to the tubing so that it can be attached to a door frame at home.

PLANT SEEDS
(INDIVIDUAL)
In Matthew 13, Jesus compares God's word to a seed. When God's word is planted in our hearts, we can grow as followers of God's way.

Materials: paper cups, potting soil, bean seeds, water
- Show children how to plant a bean seed
- Watch the beans grow over the next weeks.

TIP
To extend this craft, children can use acrylic paints to decorate terra cotta pots, then plant their seeds inside. Today's memory verse can be printed on a Popsicle stick and stuck into the soil.

WORDS IN MY HEART
(INDIVIDUAL)
Children will make a heart with today's memory verse printed inside.

Materials: photocopied message (see below), red card stock, white card stock, glue sticks, bamboo skewers, self-adhesive tiny mirrors
- Type out the memory verse in a small font. Photocopy for your group.
- Cut two hearts for each child from card stock: one white and one red.

Guide the children in the following:
- Make a window opening on the red heart, and cut this so that it opens.
- Glue hearts together, securing a bamboo skewer in between.
- Open the red heart window, and glue the memory verse onto the white background.
- Put the sticky mirror on the back of the white heart.

The message in the window can read as follows:

With my whole heart I seek you; do not let me stray from your commandments. Psalm 119:10 Look on the back to see someone God loves.

TIP
If you cannot find self-adhesive mirrors, simply omit this step and print only the memory verse inside the window.

SHEMA DOOR HANGER
Materials: photocopies of page 75 onto card stock, scissors, markers, colored pencils, hole punch, yarn

Guide the children in the following:
- Color and decorate the door hangers.
- Cut the door hangers apart and punch a hole in the top of each.
- String yarn through the hole and tie around a door knob.

Kids Move

TALENT CHARADES
(GROUP)

God has placed talents in each person. In this game, children will act out various talents or gifts for the group to guess.

Materials: talent cards

Ahead of time, make talent cards by writing on index cards words such as sing, draw, play soccer, learn piano, math, spell, read, run, gymnastics, play baseball, talk, listen, learn about nature, take care of animals, and play with younger kids.

Guide the children in the following:
- Draw a card, and act out that talent.
- The group will guess the talent.
- Continue until all have had a turn.

TIP
Make index cards based on talents that you know exist in your group. Add enough talent cards so that each person can have two turns.

ROCK, SAND, RAIN
(PARTNERS)

This game is played like "Rock, Paper, Scissors." It will help children to remember key words in today's story.

Guide the children in the following:
- Use both hands to give a signal. The signal for "rock" is two fists out in front. The signal for "sand" is two flat hands, face down, out in front. The signal for "rain" is both hands falling down, like rain showers.
- Partners say, "Rock, sand, rain," and then make their signal. Rock beats sand, sand beats rain, and rain beats rock.

LISTEN CLOSELY!
(GROUP)

It is important to listen for God's voice. In this game, children need to listen to a friend's voice to get through the obstacle course.

Materials: obstacle course, blindfolds

Ahead of time, set up a simple obstacle course of chairs, cones to walk around, or tables to crawl under.
- Divide the children into three groups.
- Group 1 puts on blindfolds.
- Group 2 shouts helpful directions to get group 1 through the course.
- Group 3 shouts unhelpful directions.
- Have the groups trade roles.

Afterward, discuss how it felt to be the group being led through the obstacle course. Was it hard to listen? We need to tune into God's voice and to tune out other voices around us that may be telling us the opposite of God's way.

STICK TO THE HEART TAG
(GROUP)

Children will play a version of "Blob tag." Just like the caught people "stick" to IT, we can memorize God's words and keep them in our hearts.

Materials: red paper heart, safety pins
- The person who is IT will wear a big, red construction paper heart.
- When IT tags someone, that person joins hands with IT to help tag others.
- Play continues until every person has been caught.

Closing
For closing ideas, see page 7.

73

"THE BIBLE IN THEIR HEARTS"
BASED ON "THE BIBLE IN THEIR HEARTS" IN *I HEARD GOOD NEWS TODAY* BY CORNELIA LEHN (FAITH AND LIFE PRESS, 1983).

Karl Olsen sold Bibles. He sold them by trudging along the muddy roads from village to village in eastern Poland.

One day, he was very tired as he struggled along the road. He approached the first house that he came to, and knocked on the door. A man answered, and Karl said, "I am in search of a place to stay tonight. I have money to pay and books to sell. I also can read and tell stories to those in whose homes I stay."

The man's children looked delighted, so the man invited Karl in.

After the family ate supper with Karl, he sat down to tell them a story. He pointed to the Bible and said, "This is the most precious book in the world." He told them the story of the good Samaritan, then said, "You have been a good Samaritan to me. You have taken me in and given me shelter." Karl told more Bible stories that night, and the children begged their father to buy a Bible for them to keep. He agreed, and from that day on, the family read stories together from their Bible.

Sometimes when they read, a neighbor would drop in. Bit by bit, the Bible stories started spreading to others in the small Polish village. On the long winter nights, people would gather to hear the stories.

They found that the stories started to change the people. They read about forgiveness, about showing kindness to others, and learned the teachings of the Bible.

Years later, Karl Olsen was walking through the same village. He decided to stop to greet the family he had met years ago. He wondered if they would recognize

him. One of the grown children answered the door, and excitedly told her mother, "Mama! It's Karl! He has come back!" The exciting news spread quickly through the village, and soon a big crowd from the village gathered around Karl.

Bit by bit, they told him their story. They showed him the Bible that he had sold them. It was almost falling apart! They told Karl that over two hundred people had become followers of Jesus just because of the message in the Bible.

The next day, they gathered for worship. Karl asked, "Is there anyone who has learned a Bible verse and would like to recite it?" Someone answered, "Chapters or verses?" Karl exclaimed, "Chapters?! Is there anyone here who knows a whole chapter of the Bible by heart?" The grownups smiled while the children giggled. "Yes!" said one man, "We were so afraid that we might lose the only Bible we had that we started memorizing it. Each boy, girl, man, and woman was assigned a part. Now we can, as a group, recite most of the books of the Bible by heart."

Karl was stunned. He thought in amazement, "Many years ago, I sold one Bible here, and this is what has come of it! When God works in the hearts and minds of people, incredible things can happen!"

"THE FAMILY BIBLE"
(author unknown)
Old Brother Higgins built a shelf for the family Bible to rest itself lest a sticky finger or grimy thumb might injure the delicate pages some. He cautioned his children to touch it not and it rested there with never a blot though the Higgins tribe were a troublesome lot. His neighbor, Miggins, built a shelf. "Come children," he said, "and help yourself." His book is old and ragged and worn, with some of the choicest pages torn, where children have fingered and thumbed and read. But of the Miggins tribe I've heard it said, each carries a Bible in his head.

<table>
<tr><td>

שְׁמַע

יִשְׂרָאֵל

יְהֹוָה

אֱלֹהֶינךָ

יְהֹוָה

אֶחָר

Hear
O Israel:
The LORD
Is our God,
The LORD
Alone

</td><td>

שְׁמַע

יִשְׂרָאֵל

יְהֹוָה

אֱלֹהֶינךָ

יְהֹוָה

אֶחָר

Hear
O Israel:
The LORD
Is our God,
The LORD
Alone

</td></tr>
</table>

Session 8
Guiding light

(8)

When we read the Bible, God can guide us. We can be inspired to change things in our lives or to live in God's ways as shown through the stories and other writings. The Bible can be like a light, leading our way.

BIBLE TEXT
Matthew 5:14-16

FAITH CHALLENGE
The Bible lights our way.

ADVANCE PREPARATION
- Read through the entire session and decide what you will do.
- Set up the room/space for the various activities.
- Gather storytelling props: flashlight, lamp, candle, nightlight, and other items that make light.
- Find enough small flashlights for each child in your group. Alternatively, use unlit birthday candles.
- Gather supplies for the craft or games you choose.
- Prepare a snack (p. 14).

Kids Cluster

1. **Plan an activity for the early arrivals.** Check page 6 for ideas.
2. **Welcome the children, and gather for a time of singing** (p. 8). Be sure to include action songs, familiar songs, favorite songs, and new songs.
3. **Begin with the theme song or an opening prayer.**
4. **Introduce today's theme:** The Bible lights our way.

Kids Dig the Bible

1. **Pass around a flashlight, lamp, candle, nightlight, and other items** that make light. Talk about what they have in common. Sometimes people are scared of the dark. Light helps to calm our fears.

   The Bible can be like our light, guiding us in God's way. We can follow the teachings of Jesus, who is called the Light of the world.

2. **Turn to Matthew 5 in your Bible.** Pass out flashlights to the children. If possible, give one to each child. If not, pass out unlit birthday candles. Tell children to hold up their light whenever they hear the word light in the story. This story is based on Matthew 5:14-16.

   Jesus said, "You are the light of the world. A big city that has been built on a hill can not be hidden. It is full of light. When someone lights a lamp, they would never put it under a bushel basket. No! They would put it up on a lamp stand so that it could light up the whole house.

   "You need to let your light shine too. Shine your light to other people so that they see the good things you have done. They will see your light and praise God."

Tip · · · · · · · · · · · ·
Use these questions/ideas as conversation points during the craft time. It is not necessary to sit quietly and reflect on these points, but do include them during other activities.

3. **Talk about the Bible**
   - In a house lit only by a candle, what would happen if that candle was blown out?
   - Imagine a city where there are no lights at night.
   - How can God's words shine through you?
   - What is the light in you?
   - How can you follow Jesus in your life and live as he taught?
   - How can the stories, poems, and rules in the Bible guide you?
   - What messages in the Bible can bring light or hope to people?
   - We can do things that blow out other people's light. What types of actions would these be (saying unkind words, making fun of someone, teasing, hitting)?

   Sing "This Little Light of Mine."

   Offer a prayer. Pass a ball or baton around the circle, with each person repeating: I could shine my light in the world by . . . *(name an action)*.

Tip · · · · · · · · · · ·
If you can find re-lighting candles, a fun activity is to light each child's candle, saying "Jesus is the light of the world." Then have them name unkind behaviors and attempt to blow out their candles after each one. They will see that the light is not extinguished, but keeps coming back. This can symbolize the strength of Jesus Christ's light.

4. **Have children recite the books of the Bible in order.** Practice today's memory verse from Psalm 119:105: "Your word is a lamp to my feet and a light to my path."

   If your group learns memory verses easily, an additional verse for today is John 8:12: "I am the light of the world. Whoever follows me will never walk in darkness but will have the light of life."

5. **Read the story "Your Word is a Light Beside Me"** (p. 85) as your group eats a snack or works at activities.

Kids Create

CANDLE HOLDERS
(INDIVIDUAL)
Materials: small glass jars, a mixture of glue thinned with water, paintbrushes, pieces of colored tissue paper, glitter, tealight candles

Guide children in doing the following:
- Use glue-and-water mixture and paintbrushes to paste pieces of tissue paper onto the outside of a small glass jar.
- Sprinkle glitter onto the glue.
- When the tealight holder dries, the light will shine through the tissue papers. Place a tealight candle in the holder for children to take home.

SIMPLE BEESWAX CANDLES
(INDIVIDUAL)
Materials: sheets of beeswax, candle wicking, scissors

Guide children in doing the following:
- Place a piece of wick across the end of a sheet of beeswax, and press firmly. The wick should be a bit longer than the sheet of beeswax.
- Roll the beeswax around the wick, slowly and steadily.
- Press the outer edge firmly to the candle.
- Trim the wick off the bottom of the candle.

STAINED-GLASS ARTWORK
(INDIVIDUAL)
For many years, artwork told the Bible stories for many people who could not read. The art of stained glass was used to decorate cathedrals and to teach people the Bible stories.

Materials: pictures of stained-glass windows, 1/8-in. / 3-mm Plexiglas sheets, fishing line, scissors, permanent markers in a variety of colors, templates (p. 83), bottle of simulated lead (*optional*)

- Ahead of time, cut Plexiglas into 4 x 6-in. / 10 x 15-cm sheets. Sand rough edges with sandpaper. Drill a small hole at the top middle for hanging.
- Show examples of stained-glass windows in churches.
- Children can create their own designs or use a template by placing it underneath the Plexiglas.

Guide children in doing the following:
- Draw design outlines with black permanent marker.
- Color in areas with colored permanent markers.
- Thread the fishing line through the hole, and knot it to make a loop.

Optional: Squeeze a line of simulated leading over the black marker outline. Let dry overnight.

CLAY LAMPS
(INDIVIDUAL)

Lamps can be a symbol of the light of God's word as it guides us along life's path. Over the years, archaeologists have found various styles of clay oil lamps that were used in Jesus' time.

Materials: newspaper, basin of water, self-hardening and fire-proof clay, candle wicking, olive oil, photocopies of note to parents (p. 81), illustrations (p. 82)

Guide children in doing the following:

- Knead a lump of clay that is about 3 in. / 7 cm in diameter for a minute or two.
- Roll clay into a ball, and press thumb into the center of the ball. Do not press all the way through.
- Make a pinch pot by forming a bowl shape, pushing and smoothing the ball with your thumbs and fingers. Work like this until all the sides are uniform, about ¼ in. / 5 mm thick.
- Bring together the opposite sides, and pinch them together so that you have two openings to your lamp, one large and one small (see diagram). Make sure to massage the pieces together carefully so that they adhere to each other.
- Set the lamp aside to dry.

Send each child home with her or his pot, a piece of wick, and a copy of this letter:

Dear parents/guardians,

This clay oil lamp your child made is patterned after first-century artifacts unearthed in the region where Jesus lived. When he told stories about hiding a lamp under a bushel or about wedding guests who forgot to bring enough oil for their lamps, Jesus may have been holding a lamp just like this one. To enjoy it safely, please note:

Though it is hardened, the clay is porous, and oils may leak through. Place the lamp on a small plate before adding oil and lighting it. Pour the oil into a separate container for storage between uses. Coil the wick inside the lamp with one end coming up through the smaller opening of the lamp. Pour ½ in. / 1 cm of cooking oil into the lamp, making sure to soak the entire wick. Vegetable oil works well. The lip of the lamp will blacken as the wick burns; that is natural. If the flame smokes, carefully use a toothpick to ease the wick lower into the lamp. If you burn the lamp for long periods, you may need to occasionally blow it out, trim the wick, and relight it.

Dear parents/guardians,

This clay oil lamp your child made is patterned after first-century artifacts unearthed in the region where Jesus lived. When he told stories about hiding a lamp under a bushel or about wedding guests who forgot to bring enough oil for their lamps, Jesus may have been holding a lamp just like this one. To enjoy it safely, please note:

Though it is hardened, the clay is porous, and oils may leak through. Place the lamp on a small plate before adding oil and lighting it. Pour the oil into a separate container for storage between uses. Coil the wick inside the lamp with one end coming up through the smaller opening of the lamp. Pour ½ in. / 1 cm of cooking oil into the lamp, making sure to soak the entire wick. Vegetable oil works well. The lip of the lamp will blacken as the wick burns; that is natural. If the flame smokes, carefully use a toothpick to ease the wick lower into the lamp. If you burn the lamp for long periods, you may need to occasionally blow it out, trim the wick, and relight it.

Kids Move

LIGHT LABYRINTH
(GROUP)

Materials: rope or sidewalk chalk, tealight candle in glass jar, music

Labyrinths have been used for many years as a way of praying and focusing on God.
Set up a simple labyrinth path ahead of time. This can be made with rope (indoors) or sidewalk chalk (outdoors). Put a lit candle in a glass jar, and place this in the middle of the labyrinth.

Play soft music in the background, and have the children walk quietly through the labyrinth one by one, leaving several paces between each person. When they get to the center, they may pause for a moment, watching the light. Then they keep going to circle back out of the labyrinth.

DARK DRAW
(SMALL GROUP)

Materials: paper, clipboards, pens or pencils
- Everyone is given a pen or pencil, and piece of paper.
- Lights are turned out, and the children are given five minutes to draw anything they want.
- Pictures can be judged for most detail, most lines, most circles, or other categories.
- If the area is not dark, children may be blindfolded.

FLASHLIGHT TAG
(GROUP)

Materials: flashlight

Play this game either indoors or outdoors, preferably with some obstacles to hide behind, such as trees, chairs, or pews.
- IT counts to twenty, then carries a flashlight to find people.
- When IT shines the light on a player, he or she is caught.
- Play continues until all players have been caught by the light.

SPOOKY SCAVENGER HUNT
(GROUP)

Materials: scavenger hunt list, flashlights, pens
- Play either indoors or outdoors in the dark.
- Make a list of things that must be found. The list could include names or information on a sign, types of cars in the parking lot, types of flower in the flower bed, and other items.
- Divide children into groups of about four or five. Each group is given a flashlight, a scavenger hunt list, and a pen.
- As the group finds an item, they cross it off the list.

TIP
For this game, enlist help from youth or other adults to travel with each group in the dark.

Closing
For closing ideas, see page 7.

"YOUR WORD IS A LIGHT BESIDE ME"

This is a true story about the Toba people, an indigenous group in Argentina. The Bible was recently translated into Toba.

When I was twenty-two years old, something unforgettable happened to me. One Saturday afternoon, we had a youth meeting in our Toba church in Argentina. We were singing together and praising God and felt such great joy. We could feel the Holy Spirit with us. We ended the meeting just when it was getting dark. We each began the walk toward our homes, down the paths, and through the fields.

As I walked through the middle of a field, feeling so happy, I glanced down at the Bible in my hand. It looked like my Bible was lit up. It was nearly dark, but my Bible shone. I looked to see where the light was coming from, but I couldn't see any source for the light. I did not feel afraid or frightened, but I wondered how this could be. I couldn't believe such a thing was really happening to me.

Right there I knelt down and prayed. I asked God to show me what this light in my Bible meant. I soon realized that God wanted me to use the Bible to guide my life. In other words, the Bible was a light to show me the way to God.

Closing celebration
Celebrating the Bible (Simchat Torah)

This celebratory session gives the children a chance to show their parents and other adults what they have been working on for the past weeks. It also gives the children and adults an opportunity to worship, create, play, and talk together. Simchat Torah is the Hebrew name for a Jewish festival when they celebrate the reading of the Torah (Genesis through Deuteronomy). During the year, the entire Torah is read. Simchat Torah, or "rejoicing in the law" in English, includes dancing with the scrolls, kissing them, and eating treats. Jesus valued the law very much, and he quoted Deuteronomy several times when he was tempted to do things he should not do.

BIBLE TEXT
Nehemiah 8:1-18

FAITH CHALLENGE
We celebrate the gift of God's word.

ADVANCE PREPARATION
- Read through the entire session and decide what you will do.
- Set up the room/space for the various activities.
- Gather storytelling props: branches, chairs, and scroll.
- Gather supplies for the craft or games you choose.
- Prepare a snack (p. 14).

Kids Cluster

1. **Plan an activity for the early arrivals.** Check page 6 for ideas.
2. **Welcome everyone, and gather for a time of singing** (p. 8). Sing favorite songs from this series that the children know well.
3. **Begin with the theme song or an opening prayer.**
4. **Introduce today's theme:** We celebrate the gift of the Bible, God's word.

Tip
If possible, provide song lyrics for adults to sing along.

Kids Dig the Bible

1. **Recite the Bible memory verses that your group has learned** during this series. Review the books of the Bible in order. Talk about the Books of the Law (Genesis through Deuteronomy) that will be mentioned in today's story.

2. **Have the group act out the story as you tell or read it.** Set out props like branches, chairs to prop branches against, and a scroll. Open your Bible to Nehemiah 8 to show where today's story comes from. This story is based on Nehemiah 8:1-18.

Long ago, the people of Israel gathered in the square of the Water Gate to hear the words of the law. The priest Ezra opened the scroll, and all the people stood up. Ezra read the scroll in a loud, clear voice, and the people began to weep when they heard the words of the law. For seven whole days, Ezra read from the book of the law.

The people heard the law: "Go out into the hills and bring back branches of olive, myrtle, palm, and other leafy trees to make booths."

So the people went out, collected branches, and constructed shelters for themselves. The people lived in these booths during the festival. Day by day, Ezra kept reading. There was great rejoicing. The people were so happy to hear Ezra read from the scroll.

3. **Talk about the Bible**
   - Why do you think the people cried when they heard Ezra read the book of the law?
   - Why were they rejoicing after seven days of hearing Ezra read from the Torah scrolls?
   - When do you get excited to listen to Bible stories?
   - Which story would you like to pass on to others?
   - When can your family read the Bible or tell Bible stories together?

Tip
Use these questions/ ideas as conversation points during the craft time. It is not necessary to sit quietly and reflect on these points, but do include them during other activities.

Response Activities

Set up a variety of stations for activities children and adults can choose to do. **Here are some suggestions:**

* Dance together

Have an adult lead the "horah," a Jewish dance. This dance has six basic steps repeated over and over. The dancers stand side by side, forming a circle. They place their hands on each other's shoulders or hold hands in the circle. **The dancers perform these steps together:**

1. Step to the right with the right foot.
2. Place the left foot behind the right foot.
3. Step right with the right foot.
4. Hop on the right foot.
5. Step to the left with the left foot.
6. Hop on the left foot.

Repeat these steps as you dance around the circle.

* Act out a favorite Bible story from this series.

Use *Fun Bible Skits 1, 2, or 3* by David M. Morrow (Scottdale, PA: Faith and Life Resources, 2005–2007).

* Make a Bible banner

Materials: mural paper with Psalm 119:105 printed in big letters, construction paper light-bulb shapes, markers, glue

Guide the children and adults in the following:
- Write or draw a favorite Bible story or verses inside the light-bulb cutouts.
- Glue the cutouts onto the mural.

* Read a favorite story
- Set out children's Bible storybooks in a comfy book nook. Adults and children can read together. See page 13 for book suggestions.

* Build a booth
Materials: large branches, corn stalks, wooden sticks, other building materials
- Build a booth like the Israelite people did.
- Sit inside to eat a snack together when the group is finished.

* Spell out the words
Materials: alphabet pretzels or alphabet cereal
- Have groups spell out a favorite memory verse from this series (see page 12).

* Tell a story
- Have an adult tell a story about how the Bible has helped during a difficult time.

* Bless the children
- Ask an elder in the congregation to bless the children, as is the custom in Simchat Torah.
- Have each child walk under a blanket or "prayer shawl" to receive the blessing.
- Use your favorite benediction, or read Numbers 6:24-26.

* Play games
- Choose favorite games from previous sessions.
- Play games from previous sessions that you did not use.

* Eat together
- Plan a simple snack of cupcakes or cookies and fruit or fruit juice.
- Serve foods typical of Bible times: dried dates, figs, pomegranates, pita bread, olives, honey, and flatbread.
- Make ice cream sundaes with toppings such as chocolate chips, bananas and coconut.
- Have a campfire with hotdogs and marshmallows.

Tip
Send home any crafts made during this series. Consider giving out My Bible Reading Chart (Scottdale, PA: Faith and Life Resources, 2006) to encourage children to continue reading their Bibles at home.

Closing

For closing ideas, see page 7.

How the Bible came to us

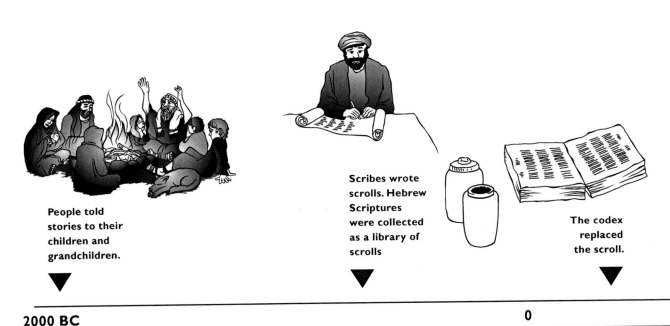

People told
stories to their
children and
grandchildren.

Scribes wrote
scrolls. Hebrew
Scriptures
were collected
as a library of
scrolls

The codex
replaced
the scroll.

▼   ▼   ▼

2000 BC   **0**

▲   ▲   ▲

Gradually
alphabets were
developed.

People learned to make
paper or parchment.

Early Christian churches
began circulating letters
written by Paul. They wrote
down accounts of Jesus' life,
death, and resurrection.

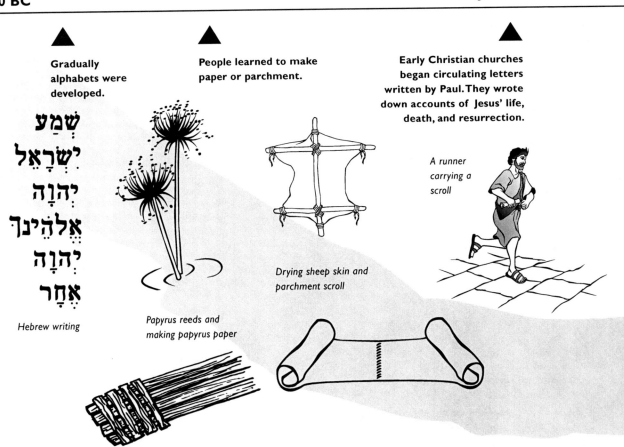

שְׁמַע
יִשְׂרָאֵל
יְהוָה
אֱלֹהֵינוּ
יְהוָה
אֶחָר

Hebrew writing

*Papyrus reeds and
making papyrus paper*

*Drying sheep skin and
parchment scroll*

*A runner
carrying a
scroll*

Jerome translated the Bible into Latin about AD 345.

Gutenberg's press

Gutenberg's Bible

Gutenberg's Printing Press. The first book printed was the Gutenberg Bible in 1456. Then more people learned to read and could own Bibles.

King James Version, 1611

AD 500   **AD 1000**   **AD 1500**   **AD 2000**

Christian leaders decided which Christian writings to use in the churches. Those were included in the Scripture. In many cases, those were the books they saved when they were hunted down and persecuted for their faith. To decide, they asked, "Does this book teach what the disciples of Jesus taught? Does this book strengthen Christians in their faith?"

The Bible was translated into many languages (Dutch, Spanish, Swedish, Danish, German, French, English, Italian). The first complete Bible printed in English was the Coverdale Bible, 1536

Discovery of the Dead Sea Scrolls, 1947

Coverdale Bible

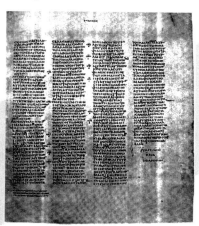

Codex Sinaiticus

Psalm Scroll

Evaluation
Tell us what you think

• •

Congregation _____

Your Name (optional) _____

Address _____

City _____ **Province/State** _____ **Code** _____

1. I have these comments about _Kids Can Dig the Bible_ regarding session components (faith challenge, kids create, kids move, etc.).

_____
_____
_____
_____
_____
_____
_____

2. I have these comments about how the program worked for us (time frame, session flow, user-friendliness, etc.)

_____
_____
_____
_____
_____
_____

Additional comments:

_____
_____
_____
_____
_____
_____

To return
• • • • • • • • • • • • •
Please make copies of this form or use the online form at www.mpn.net/kidscanclub.

Complete form and send to:
Kids Can Dig the Bible Evaluation
Faith & Life Resources
616 Walnut Ave.
Scottdale, PA 15683

Also check out:

KIDS CAN MAKE PEACE

Using Jesus as an example of how to live as a peacemaker, *Kids Can Make Peace* teaches kids how they can become peacemakers in a complex world, how they can cherish and protect the earth's natural resources, how they can resolve conflicts, and how they can cultivate a sense of inner peace.

Each week's session includes "Kids Cluster," a time for gathering, singing, and Bible memory review; "Kids Talk Peace," with a Bible story, reflection, and conversation starters on the weekly theme; "Kids Create," with hands-on crafts and response activities; and "Kids Move," featuring games that relate to the theme. Also included are suggestions for opening and closing time, snacks, and more. Materials are suitable for a variety of settings, and easily adapted to kindergarten or junior youth.

Kids Can Club is a series of all-in-one, flexible resources for children's midweek, Sunday night, camp, or other settings.

www.mpn.net/kidscanclub

CPSIA information can be obtained at www.ICGtesting.com
Printed in the USA
BVOW051852020212

282007BV00006B/2/P